LIFTING UP THE POOR

A DIALOGUE ON RELIGION, POVERTY & WELFARE REFORM

MARY JO BANE

LAWRENCE M. MEAD

BROOKINGS INSTITUTION PRESS

Washington, D.C.

Copyright © 2003
THE BROOKINGS INSTITUTION
GEORGETOWN UNIVERSITY

All rights reserved. No part of this publication may be reproduced or transmitted in any form or by any means without permission in writing from the Brookings Institution Press, 1775 Massachusetts Avenue, N.W., Washington, D.C. 20036 (fax: 202/797-6195 or e-mail: permissions@brookings.edu).

Library of Congress Cataloging-in-Publication data available
Bane, Mary Jo.
Lifting up the poor : a dialogue on religion, poverty, and welfare reform / Mary Jo Bane, Lawrence M. Mead.
    p.   cm.   — (The Pew Forum dialogues on religion and public life)
Includes bibliographical references and index.
ISBN 0-8157-0791-6 (pbk. : alk. paper)
1. Poor—United States. 2. Poverty—Religious aspects. 3. Poverty—Biblical teaching. 4. Public welfare—United States. 5. Church and social problems—United States. 6. Social justice—United States. I. Mead, Lawrence M. II. Title. III. Series.
HV91.B25 2003
261.8'325—dc22   2003020358

2 4 6 8 9 7 5 3 1
The paper used in this publication meets minimum requirements of the American National Standard for Information Sciences—Permanence of Paper for Printed Library Materials: ANSI Z39.48-1992.

Typeset in Adobe Caslon

Composition by R. Lynn Rivenbark
Macon, Georgia

Printed by R. R. Donnelley
Harrisonburg, Virginia

LIFTING UP
THE POOR

THE PEW FORUM DIALOGUES ON RELIGION AND PUBLIC LIFE

E. J. Dionne Jr., Jean Bethke Elshtain, Kayla M. Drogosz

Series Editors

THE PEW FORUM ON RELIGION & PUBLIC LIFE

This book series is a joint project of the Pew Forum on Religion and Public Life and the Brookings Institution.

The Pew Forum (www.pewforum.org) seeks to promote a deeper understanding of how religion shapes the ideas and institutions of American society. At a time of heightened interest in religion's public role and responsibilities, the Forum bridges the worlds of scholarship, public policy, and journalism by creating a platform for research and discussion of issues at the intersection of religion and public affairs. The Forum explores how religious institutions and individuals contribute to civic life while honoring America's traditions of religious liberty and pluralism.

Based in Washington, D.C., the Forum is co-chaired by E. J. Dionne Jr., senior fellow at the Brookings Institution, and Jean Bethke Elshtain, Laura Spelman Rockefeller Professor of Social Ethics at the University of Chicago. Melissa Rogers serves as executive director and Sandra Stencel as associate director. The Forum is supported by the Pew Charitable Trusts through a grant to Georgetown University.

The Pew Forum Dialogues on Religion and Public Life are short volumes that bring together the voices of scholars, journalists, and policy leaders engaged simultaneously in the religious and policy realms. The core idea behind the dialogues is a simple one: There are many authentically expert voices addressing important public questions who speak not only from their knowledge of the policy issues at stake, but also from a set of moral concerns, often shaped by their religious commitments. Our goal is to find these voices and invite them to join in dialogue.

CONTENTS

vii

FOREWORD

xi

ACKNOWLEDGMENTS

1

INTRODUCTION
E. J. DIONNE JR., JEAN BETHKE ELSHTAIN, AND KAYLA M. DROGOSZ

12

A CATHOLIC POLICY ANALYST LOOKS AT POVERTY
MARY JO BANE

53

A BIBLICAL RESPONSE TO POVERTY
LAWRENCE M. MEAD

107

A REPLY TO MEAD
MARY JO BANE

120

A REPLY TO BANE
LAWRENCE M. MEAD

Contents

140
PERSONAL RESPONSIBILITY
MEANS SOCIAL RESPONSIBILITY
MARY JO BANE

153
GUARANTEE WORK RATHER THAN AID
LAWRENCE M. MEAD

173
CONTRIBUTORS

175
INDEX

FOREWORD

I⟶'s ᴏꜰᴛᴇɴ ꜱᴀɪᴅ that two things that should not be discussed in polite company are religion and politics. If that's your view, you probably shouldn't read further—but that would be your loss. This thoughtful and lively book sheds light on an area where many scholars fear to tread: the intersection of faith and public policy.

In fact, it's impossible to make sense of either American history or contemporary politics without an understanding of the role that religion plays in public life. And it's impossible to understand religion and public life without recognizing that people of faith can, in good conscience and a civil fashion, disagree on vital public questions. In fact, they often disagree, despite sharing many beliefs and values.

Mary Jo Bane and Larry Mead are two of America's finest social scientists. They have been grappling for years with the problems of poverty and welfare. Many who have read and profited from their work may not know that Mary Jo and Larry are people of faith. Their views on the questions at hand have been vitally informed by their religious convictions.

This book recreates a searching dialogue between two people who respect each other and who are clear and honest about what they believe and why they believe it. They have accepted the late Christopher Lasch's exacting standard for constructive public debate: "We have to enter imaginatively into our opponents' arguments, if only for the purpose of refuting them, and we may end up being persuaded by those we sought to persuade. Argument is risky and unpredictable, therefore educational."

It's with that principle in mind that the Brookings Institution Press is publishing a new series of dialogues in cooperation with the Pew Forum on Religion and Public Life. The dialogues will include many participants in the debate: critics, practitioners, policymakers, public intellectuals, and religious leaders. The purpose of the Pew Forum dialogues is not to impress a particular viewpoint on readers, and it certainly is not to offer one set of answers to the questions posed—or to suggest that there is only one answer to any of those questions. Quite the contrary—in an area of public life where lines are often drawn sharply and harden quickly, the dialogues take exactly the opposite approach. They are intended to open the debate, not narrow it.

Two of the series editors, my colleague at Brookings, E. J. Dionne, and Jean Bethke Elshtain, of the University of Chicago, have embraced that outlook ever since they helped found and co-chair the Pew Forum in 2000. The third editor, Kayla M. Drogosz, has herself lived by Lasch's injunction by entering imaginatively into both Mary Jo and Larry's arguments and urging them (although it took very little prodding) to engage with their toughest critics in the worlds of public policy and theology.

Some might find it unusual for Brookings to be involved in the search for common ground between social science and religion. Not really. E. J. and another of our colleagues, John DiIulio, pointed out in their earlier Brookings volume, *What's God Got to Do with the American Experiment*, that there is a long and honorable history of engagement between the two. It ranges from Max Weber and Emile Durkheim to Will Herberg, Robert Bellah, and Andrew Greeley—and, one might add, to James Davison Hunter, Alan Wolfe, and Robert Wuthnow, among many others. In fact, this volume and the series of which it is a part reflect Brookings's growing interest in the field of religion and public life—reflecting, in turn, a quickening of interest throughout our society. Last year A. James Reichley wrote *Faith in Politics*, which grew out of his highly regarded *Religion in American Public Life*, published by Brookings in 1985. The Dionne and DiIulio volume was followed by *Sacred Places, Civic Purposes: Should Government Help Faith-Based Charity?* edited by E. J. and Ming Hsu Chen. We are delighted to continue this conversation in the dialogue series.

We are pleased as well that Mary Jo and Larry have, once again, brought their scholarly work to Brookings. In 1997 Larry edited *The New Paternalism: Supervisory Approaches to Poverty*, a study of antipoverty programs that seek to govern behavior. More recently he contributed a chapter in the book *The New World of Welfare*, edited by Rebecca Blank, dean of the Gerald R. Ford School of Public Policy at the University of Michigan, and Ron Haskins, a senior fellow in our Economic Studies department. Mary Jo has written about inner-city poverty in the Brookings volume *The Urban Underclass*, edited by Christopher Jencks and Paul Peterson. Their larger body of research has also been crucial to the Welfare Reform and Beyond project at Brookings.

Finally, as you will already have gathered, we would not have been able to do much of our work on religion and public life without the support of the Pew Charitable Trusts, an organization that has generously supported so many creative projects at our institution. The dialogues are a creation of the Pew Forum and will be part of its expanded efforts to engage civic leaders, including elected officials, in serious dialogue about the relationship between faith and public policy. As the editors put it in their introduction, "Our public deliberations are more honest and more enlightening when the participants are open and reflective about the interactions between their religious convictions and their commitments in the secular realm."

It is customary to close with a disclaimer: the opinions expressed in this volume are those of the authors alone and do not necessarily reflect the views of the Pew Forum, the Pew Charitable Trusts, or the trustees, officers, or staff of the Brookings Institution. But speaking for myself, I can say that the spirit of this book, which combines thoughtful reflection with deep knowledge, long study, and openness to the views of others, is one that we at Brookings hope to replicate in all of our scholarship and publications.

STROBE TALBOTT
President, Brookings Institution

July 2003
Washington, D.C.

ACKNOWLEDGMENTS

MARY JO BANE would like to thank Brent Coffin, Larry Mead, Thomas Massaro S.J., Martha Minow, Kenneth Winston, and Christopher Winship for comments on drafts of her essays. She also would like to thank Roger Haight S.J., Father Bryan Hehir, David Hollenbach, Robert Manning S.J., and Father Daniel Riley for helping her navigate Catholic theology.

Larry Mead gratefully acknowledges comments on earlier drafts of his essays from Gail Arnall, Brock Baker, Robin Brady, Mary Jo Bane, Brent Coffin, Tom D'Andrea, Judy Newman, Michael Novak, Michael Parker, Mark Roelofs, Joel Schwartz, Max Stackhouse, and Michael Wiseman. He also appreciates preliminary conversations about Catholic social teaching with Father Louis Cabral, Father Malcolm Kennedy, Luis Téllez, and Father Juan Velez.

Mead and Bane wish to thank E. J. Dionne and Kayla M. Drogosz for their thoughtful comments on the earliest drafts and for bringing the two of them together in dialogue.

Rebecca Rimel, the president of the Pew Charitable Trusts, and Luis Lugo, the director of its religion program, helped bring the Pew Forum to life and have generously supported its program—and also work on religion and public life at the Brookings Institution—not only by offering material help, but also by sharing their vision, wisdom, and good sense. They've shown their steadfast commitment to new ventures and have been supportive of this project in every possible way.

The editors also are extremely grateful to Strobe Talbott, president of the Brookings Institution, for his deep and energetic commitment to this project; to Carol Graham for her leadership as director of the Brookings Governance Studies Program; to Paul Light and Tom Mann for their friendship and for doing so much to make our projects possible; to Ron Haskins for his enthusiasm and encouragement; to Christina Counselman for helping in countless ways to bring this series to life; to Bethany Hase and Robert Wooley for administrative assistance; to Staci S. Waldvogel, who was present at the creation of the Pew Forum and constantly inspires us to live up to its purposes; to Inge Lockwood for proofreading; to Bob Faherty, the director of the Brookings Institution Press, who never, ever fails us, embracing our projects with deep intelligence and exceptional understanding; to Becky Clark for making sure that this publication saw the light of day; to Janet Walker and Eileen Hughes for being gifted and patient editors; and to Susan Woollen and Sese Paul Design for doing terrific work in creating the covers for the dialogue series.

We leave for last, but only for emphasis, our deep gratitude to Melissa Rogers. She has served as executive director of the Pew Forum with creativity, intelligence, insight, and understanding—and she is simply a magnificent human being. Without Melissa's tireless labor, her gift of fairness and balance, and her ability to see around corners, the seeds sewn by the Forum would have fallen on hard stones. This book frequently speaks in praise of hard work, so its patron saint might well be Sandra Stencel, the Forum's associate director. Whether dealing with ideas or budgets, books or events, scholars or consultants, Sandy makes things happen and strengthens our faith that hope and charity are possible.

Above all, the editors thank the authors of this book. May their brave and thoughtful efforts to take each other's ideas seriously move us down the path toward the truth and become a model for political dialogue in our country.

INTRODUCTION

E. J. DIONNE JR., JEAN BETHKE ELSHTAIN, AND KAYLA M. DROGOSZ

Do PROPHETS HAVE useful things to say to politicians about appropriate policies toward the poor? Do social scientists reveal truths about the causes of poverty? Can religious sensibilities clarify our thinking about poverty? To all these questions, the contributors to this volume answer Yes. The prophets have much to teach us about poverty. So do public policy specialists, and they can even be informed by their religious sensibilities.

And one more question: why would two distinguished social scientists recognized for their expertise on poverty and welfare devote their time and energy to debating the moral and religious underpinnings of our national debate over the best ways to lift up the poor and empower them to advance their own fortunes and those of their families?

The simple answer is that we asked them to, and the result is this extraordinary book, the first volume in the Pew Forum Dialogues on Religion and Public Life. But we asked, and they embraced the task, because all of us agree that debates on public policy in the United States are inevitably shaped by the moral and religious commitments of individuals and communities. As the distinguished political scientist Hugh Heclo has said: "Government policy and religious matters are not the same thing, but neither do they exist in isolation from each other. The two are distinct but not separate from each other." The two domains intertwine, Heclo says, "because both claim to give authoritative answers to important questions about how people should live."[1] Heclo's words apply especially to the issue of poverty, a matter on which the great religious traditions have much to say.

This book and the series of which it is part are built on the idea that religion always has played and always will play an important role in American public life. Religion is by no means the only factor in public policy debates. Many who come to the public square reach their conclusions on matters of import for practical and ethical reasons that have little or nothing to do with faith. Yet the religious and secular alike can agree that our public deliberations are more honest and more enlightening when the participants are open and reflective about the interactions between their religious convictions and their commitments in the secular realm.

This does not happen often enough. Some participants in public debate fear that they will be misunderstood if they talk about their faith. Many worry, understandably, that being explicit about their religious convictions and faith commitments will be misinterpreted as an attempt to impose their religious views on the unwilling. We therefore salute the courage of Mary Jo Bane and Larry Mead for kicking off this series and for being willing to bring their respective faith traditions, political commitments, and academic experience together in this moving, pointed, and informed discussion of one of the most important issues facing our nation.

All who care about welfare policy and the prospects of the poor recognize Bane and Mead as two of the most brilliant voices in our national debate about poverty. But we suspect that few who know their work also know of the importance of their religious faith to their understanding of society's obligations to the poor. Their dialogue will, we hope, encourage others to be more explicit about their underlying commitments. And their ability to combine rigorous policy analysis with serious theological reflection might serve as a model for those who believe that religious voices have much to contribute to our nation's public life. Religious Americans engage each other and those who have no religious commitments in political debate all the time. We hope that this book—and the dialogue series—will provide a service to study groups in churches, synagogues, and mosques in their efforts to understand the links between each other's religious convictions and commitments in the secular realm. For if those who care about policy need to understand the faith dimension, those who bring their faith to public life need to accept the same standards of rigor that apply to others engaged in the debate. If faith matters, so do facts, history, experience, and experimentation. Doing good is a worthy goal. More good can be done if those with good intentions pay close attention to what already works and to what might work in the future. That is why we think this book also speaks to leaders in the public policy debate, whether or not they share either Bane's or Mead's religious commitments.

Their dialogue, in fact, challenges those who automatically connect religious engagement in public life to narrow, sectarian thinking and to divisiveness and exclusion. There is nothing narrow or sectarian about this book. Bane and Mead disagree fundamentally on some things. Yet they engage each other in a spirit well described by the political philosopher Glenn Tinder when he insisted that each of us can usefully both give and receive help on the road to truth.[2] Bane emphasizes the social justice claims of the Catholic tradition, and Mead draws directly from the Bible, but both make clear that engagement with religious traditions is indispensable to a searching debate about poverty.

Where politics is concerned, some Americans automatically associate the word "religious" with the words "right" or "fanaticism." Since the late 1970s, religious conservatives certainly have played an important role in politics. But religious people are not uniformly conservative, and most are not fanatical. Many are moderate or liberal, and some place themselves on the left. Others disdain ideology. Some mistrust politics altogether.

More to the point, while religious fanatics exist and come in many political shapes and sizes, most religious people, in our experience at least, are wary of fanaticism. When they bring their faith to the public square they are thoughtful, or at least they try very hard to be. Here again, we think Bane and Mead provide a model that we hope others might emulate.

Mary Jo Bane is a professor of public policy and management at Harvard University. Where welfare is concerned, she knows whereof she speaks. She was commissioner of the New York State Department of Social Services in 1992 and 1993. From 1993 to 1996, she was assistant secretary for children and families at the U.S. Department of Health and Human Services (HHS). She is the author of many books and articles on welfare, poverty, and families, including *Welfare Realities: From Rhetoric to Reform*, coauthored with David Ellwood, her colleague at Harvard and in the Clinton administration. They argued that the old welfare system encouraged an "eligibility-compliance culture," an administrative approach more concerned with eligibility rules than with helping clients achieve self-sufficiency. Her essay here might be seen as offering some of the moral underpinnings of this view.

Like her HHS colleagues Wendell Primus and Peter Edelman, Bane resigned from the administration in 1996 after President Clinton signed the welfare reform law. "I tried to imagine myself staying in the job, implementing a law I thought was harmful, and defending it in Congressional hearings and public speeches, which I would have to do," she has written, "and I realized I simply could not do it."[3]

Lawrence Mead, a professor of politics at New York University, is the author of several influential books on poverty and welfare. He was the deputy director of research for the Republican National Committee and has held several policy and research positions in and around the federal government. He testifies regularly before Congress on poverty, welfare, and social policy issues. In *Beyond Entitlement* and later books, Mead challenged the view of welfare as an unconditional entitlement for the poor. Overcoming poverty, he asserted, required helping the poor but also changing a deeply rooted, "permissive" culture within government social programs and replacing it with work requirements and efforts to encourage other standards of good behavior. Reducing dependency, as such, was less important for Mead than changing the culture of poverty. In his view, the purpose of public policy is to get people working and to encourage a closer connection between the poor and their own communities—and ultimately with society.

Mead thinks that expectations for people on welfare have to be set mainly by the federal and state governments but that churches and other faith-based organizations have a significant role to play in program implementation. "Churches," he says, "can involve the poor in a community that is at once limitlessly giving and intensely demanding."[4] While government provides welfare benefits, congregations can enforce standards. "[I]n less formal ways, non-governmental institutions also help uphold public norms. . . . Churches and synagogues extol decency toward others, private schools promote learning, while the market economy rewards success in serving the customer."[5]

Catholic Sensibilities, Citizenship, and Democracy

"I have run large social services agencies, an activity that can make one both practical and humble," Mary Jo Bane writes. "To this analysis, as to that work, I have brought my practical experience and my social science knowledge, but I have also brought moral principles that for me have their roots in Catholic social teaching and a Catholic sensibility that is shaped every day by prayer and worship."

A practicing Roman Catholic who identifies strongly with her church's teaching on justice and the economy, Bane introduces powerful concepts in explaining the influence of her faith on her policy judgments. She speaks of her "Catholic sensibility" as something that develops, in part, from her "Catholic imagination."

Policy analysis, she writes, is often "indeterminate" and "inconclusive." It requires grappling with "competing values that must be balanced." It demands judgment calls, and Bane's Catholic sensibility informs the calls she makes. It encourages an approach that is "hopeful rather than despairing, trusting rather than suspicious, more generous than prudent, more communitarian than individualistic." For Bane, social ethics "whether secular or religious, can offer different or at least more explicit criteria for valuing one set of outcomes over others." And this balancing takes place not only in the mind of a single policy analyst, but within a deliberative community that includes many voices, both inside and outside the church.

For Bane this community relies on a body of writings about poverty and inequality drawn from Catholic social teaching. As formulated by recent popes, bishops' conferences, and theologians, this teaching emphasizes the "supreme value of human life."[6] The church has invoked the "inherent dignity of life from conception to natural death" to oppose abortion and the death penalty. But the idea also applies to society's responsibility to the poor. Catholics assert that there is a "preferential option for the poor"—an obligation to view their needs as especially important. "The Catholic tradition of respect for life," Bane writes, "leads us to conclusions that are pro-life, pro-family, and pro-poor. Anyone guided by these principles soon finds himself or herself treading uneasily upon the platforms of the two major American political parties."[7]

Catholic imagination also contributes to Bane's Catholic sensibility. Catholic imagination, for her, is the "source of an attractive set of virtues and perceptions" that are rooted in the Catholic tradition but that also are present in different ways in other world views. Drawing from the concepts of analogical and sacramental imagination developed in different ways by the Catholic thinkers David Tracy and Andrew Greeley, Bane sees the world not as sinful or God forsaken, but as "created and redeemed by a God who takes a personal interest in the well-being of men and women, a hopeful place that is basically good and in which redemption is always possible." In this framework, God is experienced in community as well as in private prayer and individual Bible reading. Interpretations of Scripture are reinforced by Catholic sensibility, which Bane describes as "intuitions about and responses to people and the world that are shaped by our sacramental imagination, liturgy and prayer."

In keeping with Catholic tradition, Bane also lays heavy emphasis on the concept of subsidiarity, which asserts that people's responsibilities to each other are best exercised at the level of social organization closest to those in need. Subsidiarity is not a doctrine of states' rights. It does not deny important federal or national responsibilities, and Bane sees an important federal role in lifting up the poor. But it is a useful reminder that treating the poor with respect requires an emphasis on the local, the specific, and the personal.

Although Bane shares Mead's commitment to work as a path to human dignity, she believes that social barriers of various sorts require caution about enforcing work requirements. She worries that recent approaches to welfare reform that seek to impose work requirements (including the 1996 bill) run the risk of punishing recipients—and their children—for circumstances beyond their control. She urges policymakers to pay attention to those causes of poverty that are rooted in discrimination, social injustices, and the accidents of life. Many people are poor not because of a lack of effort or because of their "character." The poor often suffer from the economic situation of their communities, the circumstances of the families into which they were born, or their lack of citizenship—all factors outside their control.

6

For Bane, race also is clearly a factor. Drawing from Glenn Loury's research, Bane points to discrepancies in social capital that "inhibit advancement and sometimes reinforce destructive behavior" in groups that do not have the same opportunities because of the color of their skin. Bane writes, "This in turn can induce the behavior on the part of whites that keep the disadvantaging racial conventions in place." She suggests that policies could expand access to the opportunities that "increase human capital: the education, skills, and behaviors that enhance productivity and lead to greater success in the labor market." Scriptural mandates to love one's neighbor, Bane concludes, "are not limited to the neighbor who looks like you, who lives near you, or who is a fellow citizen." This creates a moral imperative to overcome "barriers to entry or exclusion from the resources of the society."

Bane supplements her religious commitments by drawing on the work of other social scientists, applying, for example, the economist Amartya Sen's understanding of poverty in the developing world to the United States. Sen focuses on expanding substantive or "real freedoms" that enable humans to flourish in the broadest sense. He sees poverty as "the deprivation of basic capabilities rather than merely as lowness of income." Despite the secular roots of Sen's analysis, Bane finds it more congruent with the Catholic conception of the human person than conventional measures of poverty based on income. Bane's analysis points to policies that seek to increase capabilities or alleviate "capability deprivation."

"By focusing on capabilities rather than substantive outcomes," she writes, we respect personal choices while preserving the "rights and responsibilities of human persons to develop and use the gifts that are their legacy from their Creator." This view implies not only the imperative to provide work opportunities for the poor, but also the chance to participate more fully in society as a whole, including in politics, the art of self-rule. Interestingly, Bane's faith-based definition of the good life closely parallels the philosopher Judith Shklar's assertion that the dignity of work and personal achievement lie "at the very heart of American civic self-identification."[8] "The opportunity to work and to be paid an earned reward for one's labor was a social right," Shklar says, "because it was a primary source of public respect."[9] In this understanding, work is both an obligation and a right that society must foster and protect.

Common Moral Principles in a Pluralist Society

Lawrence Mead shares with his co-author the view that citizens—and especially believers—have a clear duty to the poor, a responsibility that is shared by individuals and the government. Mead's essays here discuss the nature of these obligations and how they can mutually reinforce one another. He also believes that theology has much to contribute to public policy. "Theologians who address poverty believe they are powerless," he writes. "They say government ignores them. But church teachings about social ethics shape what society thinks 'doing good' for the poor means. Like the poets Shelley spoke of, theologians are among the 'unacknowledged legislators of mankind.'"

Mead's theological viewpoint is quite different from Bane's. He writes as a Protestant influenced by a view of scripture that is personal rather than rooted in a church tradition. He criticizes Bane's "Catholic sensibility" and Catholic social teaching. He sees the New Testament's narrative of "salvation" as restoring individuals to full moral agency. Jesus, he says, responds to the poor but also expects good behavior from them, and government should do the same. The ideal is to create a community to which both rich and poor contribute. The poor, like other people, should be forgiven their failures, but also challenged to live better. It is worth noting that Mead's approach is not meant to be exclusionary. He argues passionately for its universal application. The principles he describes are meant to be acceptable by all and applicable to all.

For Mead, nurturing personal responsibility and other virtues that Christians celebrate is central to fighting poverty and is at the core of being a good citizen. He also identifies a deep public concern for the poor in his tradition and argues that even nonbelievers can look to the Christian tradition as "the crucible that formed the moral values of modern politics." Welfare policy, in turn, can be the crucible that strengthens—or diminishes—citizenship.

Like Shklar, Mead sees those without work as being beyond the pale of society. "In the biblical tradition," Mead writes, "concern is at least as great for the separation of the poor from mainstream society" as it is for finding structural solutions to economic poverty. "The poor are not simply needy, they are *outcasts*. This is because they are seen to have violated social mores, reflecting the same concerns about 'deservingness' that still surround poverty today." Poor adults must work if they are to enter the community. But where Shklar treats work as a right that society must guarantee, Mead treats it as an obligation that the poor owe to society in return for what it gives them.

Like Bane's, Mead's position also rests on a certain reading of the social science evidence about poverty. He doubts that lack of work, and hence poverty, among working-age adults can be explained by social barriers. Mead writes in the tradition of those who see a culture of poverty. The poor, he says, "want to work, maintain their families, and so on. But they feel unable to do so in practice. They perceive myriad obstacles outside themselves that make them unable to work."[10] The culture of poverty, he argues, must be broken by overcoming a "defeatist culture." He worries that past failures lead poor people to internalize a paralyzing sense of hopelessness, fatalism, and despair. These, in turn, breed a lack of self-discipline and commitment to the future.

In contrast to Bane, Mead challenges the view of many in the Christian churches who see *economic* poverty as a biblical priority that deserves "preference ahead of other social concerns." The New Testament, Mead insists, gives little warrant for this view. He challenges the premise that there is a preferential option for the poor, that economic poverty is of paramount concern, and the poor are to be helped without expectations. "There is no preference for the poor, only a lively concern for them as well as other people in trouble. Jesus does help the needy and commands his followers to do so, but he has other concerns, which are not economic, and he is not undemanding toward those he helps." Mead would encourage a reciprocal relationship between society and the poor by establishing a new social contract. This would lead to a stronger sense of citizenship on the part of both those who are poor and those who are not. "Just as the political world needed a more civic form of conservatism," he writes, "so theologians need a more civic conception of what helping the poor means."

This argument for reciprocity is at the center of Mead's bold thesis on paternalism. He uses this term to characterize increased supervision and regulation of the lives of those who receive public assistance. "The idea of paternalism is a modified version of the general idea of social contract," he said in a recent interview. "If you receive benefits, you accept some obligations in return."[11] Under Mead's vision of paternalism—much of which is embodied in the welfare reform of the 1990s—welfare programs are no longer merely instruments for delivering benefits. They are based on requirements for the poor: to work, to accept job training, to keep their children in school, to make sure they receive proper vaccinations. Paternalism emphasizes the obligations of the recipients, not just their needs and rights. Mead's policy analysis is buttressed by his own close reading of Scripture. He borrows a phrase found in the Episcopal Book of Commom Prayer, God's "service is perfect freedom," and concludes that "those who would be free must first be bound." In short, Mead's call is a call for tough love, a demanding compassion, and a belief that everyone must serve.

Secular Reasoning and the Religious Imagination

That two brilliant social policy analysts operating out of a shared religious tradition could engage in the argument contained in these pages tells us several important things. What they agree on—the urgency of assisting the poor, the importance of community, the value of work, the centrality of citizenship and responsibility—suggests grounds for potential consensus. What they disagree on or, more precisely, where their emphases differ—notably on the extent to which the causes of poverty are primarily individual or social—points to why consensus is so difficult to achieve.

But the very fact that a dialogue rooted in faith has so much to say to a secular audience points to the importance of broadening our community of deliberation by making our most deeply held commitments, beliefs, and assumptions—and, yes, biases—explicit. For the believer and the nonbeliever alike, moral reasoning is informed by emotions (for example, gratitude, trust, hope), by affections (love, friendship), and by dispositions (responsibility, generosity, accountability). In wrestling with each other's positions and commitments, Bane and Mead allow all who enter into their conversation the chance to sort out for themselves why they believe what they believe about poverty and its alleviation. Thus does the religious imagination offer a gift to secular discourse.

One last point. Mead cites Ron Sider, the thoughtful and forceful evangelical thinker who has declared that if the affluent "do not feed the hungry and clothe the naked, they go to hell."[12] Mead's view is more nuanced, but he notes that "it is a chilling prospect that few in government have dared to question." At the least, to use the language of social science, Sider's view certainly broadens the range of incentives to which politicians and policymakers might respond.

Notes

1. Hugh Heclo, "An Introduction to Religion and Public Policy," in Hugh Heclo and Wilfred McClay, eds., *Religion Returns to the Public Square: Faith and Policy in America* (Johns Hopkins University Press, 2003).

2. "A society in which people listen seriously to those with whom they fundamentally disagree—an attentive society—is the proper setting for freedom," writes Tinder. "An attentive society would provide room for strong convictions, but its defining characteristic would be widespread willingness to give and receive assistance on the road to truth." Glenn Tinder, "The Spirit of Freedom: To Live Attentively," in Richard John Neuhaus and George Weigel, eds., *Being Christian Today* (Washington: Ethics and Public Policy Center, 1992), pp. 152–53.

3. Mary Jo Bane, "Autobiographical Statement," Commonweal Colloquium, Union Theological Seminary, April 20–22, 2001.

4. Lawrence Mead, "The Poverty Debate and Human Nature," in Stanley Carlson-Thies and James Skillen, eds., *Welfare in America: Christian Perspectives on a Policy in Crisis* (Grand Rapids, Mich.: Eerdmans Publishing, 1996), p. 234.

5. Ibid., p. 237.

6. Mary Jo Bane and Thomas Massaro, "Compassion in Action: A Letter to President Bush on Social Policy," *America* (March 2002), pp. 12–15. See also Bane, "Autobiographical Statement."

7. Ibid.

8. Judith Shklar, *American Citizenship: The Quest for Inclusion*, Tanner Lectures on Human Values, University of Utah, May 1–2, 1989.

9. Ibid.

10. Lawrence Mead, "Welfare Reform and the Family," *Family Matters* (Spring–Summer 1999), pp. 12–17.

11. David Fischer, "An Interview with Lawrence Mead," Center for an Urban Future, June 18, 2002 (http://www.nycfuture.org/content/reports/report_view. cfm?repkey=75 [July 17, 2003]). The interview was conducted in early May 2002.

12. Ronald J. Sider, *Rich Christians in an Age of Hunger: Moving from Affluence to Generosity* (Nashville, Tenn.: W Publishing, 1997), p. xiv.

A CATHOLIC POLICY ANALYST
LOOKS AT POVERTY

MARY JO BANE

[Jesus] went to Nazareth, where he had been brought up, and on the Sabbath day he went into the synagogue, as was his custom. He stood up to read, and the scroll of the prophet Isaiah was handed to him. Unrolling it, he found the place where it is written:

> The Spirit of the Lord is on me,
> because he has anointed me
> to proclaim good news to the poor.
>
> He has sent me to proclaim freedom for the prisoners
> and recovery of sight for the blind,
> to release the oppressed,
> to proclaim the year of the Lord's favor.

Then he rolled up the scroll, gave it back to the attendant, and sat down. The eyes of everyone in the synagogue were fastened on him. He began by saying, "Today this scripture is fulfilled in your hearing."

LUKE 4:16–21[1]

FROM THE TIME of Jesus in the synagogue at Nazareth to the present day, Christians have proclaimed a mission to the poor and the oppressed. Their witness and their actions have been only intermittently and partially effective. As is obvious, the conditions of which Jesus spoke have not disappeared.

Religious voices today speak in a complex policy environment in which the simple message of Jesus must contend with complicated demographics, many-faceted institutional and governmental structures, and divisive politics. Sometimes their advocacy is platitudinous, sometimes contentious. Sometimes, indeed, the distinctiveness of the religious voice is hard to discern.

The purpose of this chapter is twofold. First, it presents an analysis of poverty and welfare in the United States in the early twenty-first century and offers policy recommendations on a number of issues, including welfare reform. The analysis relies heavily on empirical evidence but also presents both religious and secular philosophical arguments for its conclusions. Second, the chapter offers an example of the use of religious resources—in this case, Catholic scriptural interpretations, social teachings, and the sensibilities embedded in Catholic liturgy and tradition—in policy discourse. It is meant to show that religious language and concepts can enrich policy analysis, without excluding other voices or claiming immunity from argument.[2]

Policy analysis is sometimes thought of as a technical discipline in which judgments are based on empirical evidence analyzed to assess costs and benefits. But analysis, even in its most technical form, also incorporates human values and judgment. Policy analyses done by economists are, by and large, utilitarian in their philosophical underpinnings, and they therefore tend to favor the maximization of individual preferences as the criterion for decisionmaking.[3]

Social ethics, whether secular or religious, can offer different or at least more explicit criteria for valuing one set of outcomes over others. This analysis uses Catholic social teaching as a moral framework for analysis, showing its similarities to other ethical perspectives, to complement social science tools. It attempts to illustrate that some moral framework is always present in policy analysis and that making the moral framework explicit is more honest and helpful than assuming that the underlying moral values are universally shared. By showing the similarities of Catholic social teachings to liberal and communitarian perspectives, it offers what I hope readers will find to be a persuasive framework, or at least one that is understandable in secular as well as religious language.

The analysis also is framed by what I call the Catholic sensibility, a stance toward the world that at its best is hopeful rather than despairing, trusting rather than suspicious, more generous than prudent, more communitarian than individualistic. The stance of the analyst or decision-maker is important in the many instances in which neither ethical nor policy analysis leads to a clear answer and the person making the decisions must decide on which side to err or which assumption to give the benefit of the doubt. I offer the Catholic imagination as the source of an attractive set of virtues and perceptions with many similarities to other religious, or simply human, outlooks.

Catholic Social Teachings

Because of the centralized, hierarchical structure of the Catholic Church, it is possible to speak of church teachings, independent of the expressed opinions of Catholics or individual theologians, more securely than in other religious traditions. The social teachings of the Catholic Church are documents of the church's magisterium, or teaching authority, which in Catholic ecclesiology rests with the bishops and, as first among equals, with the Pope, who is bishop of Rome.[4] These documents are not considered to be infallible or immutable,[5] but they do represent official church teachings and are meant to be accorded deference and respect by the Catholic faithful after serious and prayerful reflection. The official social teachings come from several sources: the documents of Vatican Council II, especially the Constitution on the Church and the Modern World; papal encyclicals from the time of Leo XIII, an important recent example of which is Pope John Paul II's Centesimus Annus: *On the Hundredth Anniversary of* Rerum Novarum; and statements formally approved by councils of bishops—in the United States, by the National Conference of Catholic Bishops, especially their 1986 letter on economic justice for all.[6]

The content and style of these documents reflect both the scriptural and the natural law tradition in the moral theology of the Catholic Church. The church believes that God speaks to humanity through Sacred Scripture, human reason and experience, and the work of the

Spirit in history. The natural law tradition articulates what are meant to be universal ethical principles discerned by reflection on the truths inculcated by God in the hearts of men and women in the context of human experience. These principles are meant to be acceptable to and accepted by all, not just Catholics or Christians. The major documents of the social teachings also make use of Scripture, but they are written mostly in the language of secular philosophy and to some extent social science. They tend to be analytic in their logic, deriving more or less specific prescriptions from general principles and from consideration of specific situations and issues. They vary in their use of empirical or social scientific evidence. They also vary in their level of specificity. They sometimes articulate concrete policy conclusions; they often remain relatively general; and they occasionally, as in the American bishops' letters on peace and on the economy in the 1980s, advocate specific policies while noting that different conclusions could be legitimately derived from the principles.

The documents that make up the social teachings are used by Catholic organizations that lobby federal and state governments on behalf of Catholics—at the national level, the National Conference of Catholic Bishops, the U.S. Catholic Conference, and Catholic Charities USA. These organizations advocate very specific policies on specific legislation that are based on staff interpretations of the social teachings (and the interests of the Catholic Church as an institution) and overseen by representatives of the bishops. Catholic lobbyists on issues of poverty and welfare rely particularly on *Economic Justice for All*, the 1986 pastoral letter of the National Conference of Catholic Bishops.[7] In this volume I distinguish the social teachings per se from their use in prescribing specific policies and in lobbying efforts.[8]

Catholic social teachings, like some secular philosophies, begin with a basic commitment to the equal dignity of all men and women as creatures of God; to the notion that human flourishing must be worked out in community; and to the proposition that all God's gifts are to be used for the good of all humanity. They also articulate a special concern and love for the poor and the oppressed and a commitment to the promotion of justice. Other principles derive from the basic commitments: for example, basic human rights; the right to private property; concern for participation in governance; and limited support for a market economy, conditioned on

the need for government intervention in the market to protect the interests of the poor and vulnerable.[9] Catholic social teachings also articulate
the concept of subsidiarity, which holds that human needs should be met
by those institutions and groups that are smallest in scale and closest to
the individual that can meet those needs effectively. To a great extent,
these commitments can be and are articulated in secular language, reflecting the Catholic belief that God works through human reason.

It is worth noting at this point that not all of the many documents that
make up Catholic social teachings are completely consistent with each
other. Not only have the ideas evolved over time, but different authors have
emphasized one or another theological theme and also have differed in their
interpretations of the specific circumstances and needs of the times in which
they wrote. Individual documents have been criticized by some Catholics as
misinterpreting Scripture, Catholic tradition, natural law, or common sense.
Alternative visions and especially alternative policy conclusions have come
from both the political left and right. The American bishops' 1986 letter on
the economy, for example, generated extensive discussion.[10] From the left,
advocates of liberation theology argued with the bishops' tacit consent to
the basic framework of market capitalism and with their incremental policy conclusions. From the right, writers such as Michael Novak, whose
social ethics are more individualistic and market-friendly, contended that
the bishops had gone too far in their acceptance of the welfare state.[11] To a
large extent, the disagreements turn on facts and predictions and on differences in emphasis rather than on theology, although there are some theological disagreements as well. These criticisms show that there is some room
for dissent, on some issues, within the Catholic tradition (although some
ordained liberation theologians were disciplined and removed from pastoral
or teaching posts because of their positions). My interpretation of Catholic
social teachings here is inevitably my own, but it is meant to be a fair reading of what the documents actually say.

The Catholic Sensibility

In addition to the social teachings, Catholics bring other resources,
including what I am calling a Catholic sensibility, to policy analysis. All
religions encompass not just cognitive beliefs but also stories, rituals, and

practices embedded in prayer, worship, and community life that influence the way believers see the world, relate to it emotionally, and act in and on it. Secular world views also have important noncognitive components, notions of what the world is like, what is good, and how human beings ought to act. These dispositions and attitudes inevitably influence policy thinking and ought, I suggest, to be explicit.

The Catholic interpretation of Scripture, especially the gospels, and the Catholic sacraments, especially the Eucharist, shape the way Catholics see the world. The Catholic sacramental imagination, a concept elaborated by Andrew Greeley, sees the world as created and redeemed by a God who takes a personal interest in the well-being of men and women, as a hopeful place that is basically good and in which redemption is always possible.[12] It experiences God in community, primarily through the communal celebration of the Eucharist rather than through private prayer or individual Bible reading. It sets forth a compassionate, inclusive, and peaceful Jesus—who loved, healed, and forgave indiscriminately—as a model for living, and it calls believers to a life of discipleship as followers and imitators of Jesus.

Here, too, it is worth noting that my characterization of Catholic sensibility can be and has been contested, since individuals construct their identities through contact and interaction with a variety of people in a variety of social contexts. Some Catholics and some Catholic communities are exclusive, intolerant, and judgmental, emphasizing those elements of the Christian story that portray God in relation to a chosen elect and that see God as a stern judge of the world who holds men and women accountable for their conformity to God's law. In some cases this stance is simply mean, but in others it comes from a genuine concern that right beliefs be protected and that virtue be enforced in a sinful world. That is not my stance, and it is not, I believe, authentically Catholic, but it certainly exists within the tradition.

Policy decisionmaking inevitably relies not just on ethical and empirical analyses but also on individuals' sensibilities, perceptions, and styles of action. These are important additional resources because so much of policy analysis is indeterminate or inconclusive, resting on competing values that must be balanced; on inconclusive empirical evidence that must be assessed and weighed; or on predictions, which are inherently uncertain.

Judgment calls are inevitable, with policymakers often having to decide where to place the burden of proof or on which side to err. These judgment calls and underlying stances are shaped by our sensibilities—sometimes simply human, sometimes religious, sometimes Christian, sometimes more specifically Catholic.

My analysis brings the resources of Catholic social teachings and sensibilities to the question of poverty and welfare in the contemporary United States. In the next sections, I show how Catholic resources can shape the conceptualization of the challenge of poverty and of the locus of responsibility for dealing with poverty. In later sections, I deal more specifically with alternative policy approaches. Throughout the analysis, I show the commonalities of and differences between Catholic and other approaches.

The Challenge of Poverty

Policy analysis typically begins with a statement of the problem, usually articulated in quantitative terms, that assumes a shared set of values. For example, discussions of poverty often present data on low-income families and individuals collected by the U.S. Census Bureau and assume, usually without argument, that income poverty is a condition about which Americans should be concerned.

Catholic social teachings, like those of other religious and ethical traditions, begin explicitly with an appreciation of the preciousness of every human life and with the belief that each person is a child of God, created in God's image, and a brother or sister to every other person. Every human life has multiple dimensions and desires—material, social, and spiritual. God's plan for humanity looks to the full development of human personhood and provides the resources for the growth of God's kingdom on earth. An understanding of the "problem of poverty" in the Catholic tradition privileges the experience and aspirations of those uniquely precious men and women whom we categorize as poor, by one set of criteria or another. It attempts to understand and aggregate their complicated stories, keeping in mind both their individuality and their commonality.

Statistics can help with the aggregation. But statistics begins with definitions and too easily reifies concepts that may have been adopted simply as measurement tools. Comparing two definitions of poverty in common use among academics may help clarify this issue and alert us to a fuller conception of human personhood and development.

The definition of poverty used in the official reports and by most American researchers is based on notions of material deprivation, and it attempts to define the level of income that is necessary for a minimally decent life in the contemporary United States. Formulated in the mid-1960s, the definition of poverty is based on the cost of a nutritionally sufficient diet and on a multiplier calculated from the percentage of income that families typically spend on food. It varies by family size but not by regional or metropolitan variations in the cost of living. In 2001 the official income poverty level was $14,269 a year for a family of three and $18,104 for a family of four.[13]

This concept of income poverty is extremely useful for counting and describing the characteristics of those who fall below the poverty line that it defines. The official statistics tell us, for example, that in 2001, 32.9 million Americans lived in a household whose income was below the poverty level. That is a poverty rate of 11.7 percent. Poverty rates for Americans vary with overall movements of the economy. The poverty rate in 2000, 11.3 percent, was at its lowest since 1972; the increase between 2000 and 2001 reflects the slowdown of the economy. Poverty rates for different groups help us understand both who in America is most vulnerable to income poverty and what correlates of income poverty might explain trends and changes.

An alternative concept of poverty developed by the economist Amartya Sen is used extensively in understanding poverty in the developing world. In several aspects it is, I believe, more consistent with the Catholic conception of the human person than is the official U.S. poverty definition, and it provides an alternative approach to defining and characterizing the challenge of poverty.

Sen defines development as "a process of expanding the real freedoms that people enjoy."[14] Substantive freedoms, or capabilities, enable people to lead the kind of life they have reason to value. Sen then defines poverty as "the deprivation of basic capabilities rather than merely as lowness of income."[15] Sen's basic idea (not, by the way, derived from religious beliefs) is that human development consists in exercising human capabilities and in being able to pursue a satisfying life path. Sen identifies as especially important "elementary capabilities like being able to avoid such deprivations as starvation, undernourishment, escapable morbidity and premature mortality, as well as the freedoms that are associated with being literate and numerate, enjoying political participation and uncensored speech and so on."[16]

Freedom, according to Sen, involves both processes and opportunities. It requires, for example, processes that guarantee civil rights and adequate opportunities for functioning in society. Basic capabilities, then, include health and appropriate education—in addition to at least a minimal level of safety and of material goods—and social structures based on equal respect and opportunities for participation. Poverty comes from being deprived of these basic capabilities, which enable an individual to choose a valued way of living.

The United Nations Development Program (UNDP) has attempted to operationalize these concepts in a definition of human poverty that allows poverty to be measured for countries and includes the following: premature mortality, illiteracy, childhood malnutrition, lack of access to health services, and lack of access to safe drinking water. These indicators turn out not to be particularly well correlated with standard economic measures—for example, with per capita income or even with the standard income poverty measure of $1 or $2 a day per person, which is commonly used for defining poverty in the developing world. That fact suggests that policy might be appropriately directed at the various dimensions of human poverty, not just income poverty, and that it might be useful to expand our conception of human flourishing.[17]

The definition of human poverty used in the developing world is not particularly relevant in the United States, since the basic goods of literacy, safe drinking water, and long life (compared with life expectancy in the rest of the world) are nearly universal. A more relevant conception of human poverty that includes the capabilities necessary to participate and flourish in this society has not been systematically developed for the United States. It seems clear, however, that such a conception would be more consistent with the notions of personhood that emerge from Christian and other ethical traditions. It would recognize that a good life is not defined solely, if at all, by material well-being and that an important aspect of a good life is that it be chosen—and therefore that opportunities and processes ought to be emphasized more than physical goods.

The Christian conception of the good life is, of course, defined in a way that Sen's is not. For Sen, the good life is that which is valued by the person, although he limits the definition by adding that there must be reason to value the person's conception. For Christians, the good life is one freely lived in conformity with God's plan for humanity. Christians place less emphasis on income and wealth as aspects of the good life and more emphasis on living in right relationship to God and all God's creation in communities of peace, justice, and love, giving of one's self to others. Christians emphasize the values of continuing God's creative and saving work in the world by nurturing new life, building communities that prefigure the kingdom of God, and acting as generous stewards of God's gifts. For Christians, poverty would be seen as the deprivation of the societal structures and personal opportunities to live out God's plan.

There is much overlap of Sen's conception of poverty and that of Christians. Both see poverty as the inability to lead a good life, defined by Christian teachings for all Christians and by the individual in Sen's conception. Both see income and wealth as instrumental to living a good life, not as goods in themselves. Both see freedom as crucial—the freedom to choose a good life or to live in conformity with God's plan. Both see the development of each person's skills and abilities as crucial—to living a life worth living or to the furthering of God's kingdom. Both also see that human life is lived in society and that opportunities for inclusion and participation are key human necessities.

The challenge of poverty in America, I contend, lies in the fact that some Americans lack one or more of the important capabilities necessary for human flourishing in this society—they lack income, or opportunities to work, or opportunities to participate fully in society. This view of poverty respects the religious commitment to the equality of all human persons by its claim that no American should be deprived of these basic capabilities. It respects the preciousness of human life in its myriad dimensions, by focusing on both a range of substantive freedoms and a range of necessary capabilities, not just material well-being and the ability to achieve it. By focusing on capabilities rather than substantive outcomes, it respects the rights and responsibilities of human persons to develop and use the gifts that are their legacy from their Creator and it protects their ability to make choices. It leads to the next questions, which have to do with ways of alleviating capability deprivations.

Assessing Policy Options

Standard policy analysis tends to use efficiency or cost effectiveness as a major criterion for evaluating alternative approaches. Other considerations come into play as well—for example, operational feasibility and political support—and many policy analyses also look explicitly at the criteria of equality and participation. The assessment of costs and benefits remains central, however, partly because other more substantive values—equality, for example, or benefit to the least advantaged—are hard to agree on or to assign priority to in the secular political context.

A religious sensibility does not deny the importance of the careful use of resources. Indeed, good stewardship of the earth's resources, as of all the gifts of the Creator, is a fundamental value. But a Catholic sensibility would look to other values as well, nearly all of which have been articulated by secular thinkers but take on special relevance in an analysis informed by the Catholic tradition.

The definition of poverty as capability deprivation calls attention to all the dimensions of human flourishing, not just material well-being. This implies that the effects of policies should be assessed along a number of dimensions:

—Opportunities to work, to participate in society, and to grow intellectually, emotionally, and spiritually are as important as material well-being. The goal of policy should be to ensure the capacities necessary for human flourishing. Because human life is inevitably and rightly worked out in society, inclusion and participation are important criteria for judging policies.

The Catholic tradition also speaks to the issues of mutual responsibility, stance toward the poor, and the role of government, which lead to three additional principles that should inform any assessment of policies to address poverty:

—All people have responsibility for each other's well-being. Everyone should have opportunities to meet their responsibilities and to contribute to society, and everyone should be encouraged and in appropriate situations required to do so.

—Policies should reflect a preference for the poor and the vulnerable in keeping with biblical mandates for justice and with inclusive notions of community.

—Because of the importance of small groups and communities, there should be a preference in policymaking for private action, voluntary groups, and lower levels of government, when these lower levels can be effective in achieving the common good. But when they cannot, higher levels of government are obliged to act.

Each of these principles has secular analogues, which I examine briefly:

—Mutual responsibility. In addressing questions of responsibility, Christian social ethics begins by reflecting on God's plan for humanity as revealed in Scripture.[18] God created men and women in God's own image: creative, loving, and self-giving. Both the material world and the energy, intelligence, and talents of humans are gifts from God, to be used in accordance with God's plan. That plan is for all humanity to become a holy people, living in love of God and of one another.

The Christian gospels expand these notions in their descriptions of the teachings and actions of Jesus, who clearly emphasized the responsibilities of all. Jesus made it plain that misfortune was not to be interpreted as punishment for sins and that material wealth was not to be interpreted as reward for virtue. At the same time, Jesus called on all, rich and poor, to repent and forgave the sins of all; he implied neither that the poor were sinless nor that the rich were irredeemable. Jesus performed a number of miracles that restored the ability of those cured to participate in the community: he drove out devils; cured blindness, deafness, and lameness; and restored the sick to health. He set the example in his own work of restoring capabilities to those who had been deprived of them, and after doing so, of expecting them to exercise those capabilities for the good of the community.

The community to which Jesus called disciples was inclusive, especially of the poor and the outcasts of his day. Jesus' teachings emphasized the blessedness of the poor and the woes of the rich, but in dealing with individual men and women he "looked with love" on the rich, on tax collectors, and on state and temple officials. Jesus instructed his disciples to love their enemies and to treat all in need as their neighbors. Though Christians have not always followed the example of Jesus, Christian teachings emphasize an inclusive, indeed global, community and the responsibility of all humans for each other.

Catholic social teachings affirm both the right to private property and limits on that right that derive from what the church calls the original common destination of created goods: the requirement that God's gifts be used for the good of all. Pope John Paul II, for example, has both denounced socialism and also made powerful arguments about the obligations of the rich toward the poor.[19]

Equal dignity, mutual responsibility, and the notion that scarce resources are to be used for the common good also are features of some secular ethical writing. John Rawls, for example, argues that the advantages that enable people to succeed in society—talents, skills, resources—are largely undeserved and that therefore it is unfair for individuals to be able to benefit from them at the expense of others. This does not lead Rawls to argue that goods must be held in common, but instead that just social structures tolerate inequalities only when they work to improve the position of the least advantaged.[20]

Communitarian writers stress the obligations of both rich and poor to develop their talents and to contribute to development and good order in society by taking responsibility for themselves, their families, and their communities.[21] Their belief that the essential dignity of every human person brings with it responsibility for the well-being of others is consistent with Christian notions of God's plan for humanity. It complements the notion that a common humanity also entails opportunities for all to participate—to contribute to and to benefit from the community's gifts.

—A preference for the poor. Within the context of community and mutual responsibility, Christians teach that there is a special responsibility for the poor, the vulnerable, and the marginalized, a special preference that is to be given to them.[22] God became human in Jesus in a relatively poor and exploited province of the first-century Roman Empire. During his public life as a poor itinerant prophet, healer, and teacher, Jesus lived among the poor. He taught that the poor were blessed and that it would be difficult for the rich to enter the kingdom of heaven.[23] Jesus' ministry of healing was primarily to the poor.

Jesus, like the Hebrew prophets before him, condemned injustice and exploitation and proclaimed a kingdom of God characterized by peace, justice, and forgiveness. He was crucified as a political criminal, indicating that the Roman authorities and their Jewish collaborators feared that he was becoming the leader of a rebellion against the Romans' oppressive rule. This theme in Jesus' teaching has been developed, especially by liberation theologians, to sanction opposition to exploitative structures and regimes. On the other hand, Jesus himself addressed human misfortune primarily through acts of personal compassion and charity. Jesus praised the Samaritan who helped his neighbor and condemned the rich man who ignored the beggar Lazarus at his door. Jesus taught and demonstrated the obligation of personal charity, to the extent of stating that to achieve perfection one must sell one's possessions and give them to the poor.

Jesus reprimanded the religious and civic leaders of his day for their lack of humanity and compassion but did not explicitly speak against the oppressive policies of the Roman Empire or call for political or social revolution. Jesus was nonviolent himself, and he advocated nearly unlimited forgiveness of offenses, including those committed by the authorities. What is undeniable about Jesus' life and teachings, however, is that they exemplify a radical identification with and compassion for the poor.

Secular ethical traditions also call attention to the poor. Many utilitarians construct an argument that the principle of maximizing overall welfare requires that those who have less of a good such as income get more of an incremental increase in income, since a given amount of money will increase their overall utility more than it would that of someone who has more to start with.[24] In the liberal tradition, John Rawls argues that a just society would adhere to the "difference principle," which holds that inequalities are justified only to the extent that they benefit the least advantaged.[25] He argues that this principle would be agreed to by reasonable people in constructing principles of justice if they did not know what their own position would be within the society. Neither Christians nor liberals have a monopoly on compassion or concern, nor does either group have privileged knowledge about how best to alleviate the capability deprivations of the poor. But both approaches give us a mandate and a way of thinking about a special responsibility for the poor.

—Personal charity, intermediary institutions, and the state. Jesus' example and teachings certainly emphasized personal charity toward the poor rather than political or social organizing. Compassion, generosity, and personal charity are emphasized in the Catechism of the Catholic Church and in innumerable Sunday homilies.

The social teachings of Pope John Paul II have strongly criticized socialist solutions to the problem of poverty and have offered a qualified endorsement of market economies both as institutional mechanisms for accommodating the important human freedoms to produce and to exchange and as efficient mechanisms for development. John Paul II has warned against overintrusive "welfare states" that sap human creativity and energy. He praises family, community, and church charity and concern for the poor.[26]

Catholic social teachings, however, also emphasize the role of government and the importance of "faithful citizenship" in the context of "subsidiarity."[27] This body of teachings developed over time as theologians, church leaders, and Catholic laity read the signs of the times and attempted to apply both biblical insights and rational ethical analysis to current problems. The logic of Catholic social teachings starts with the equal dignity of human persons and with the interconnectedness of the human community. We have responsibilities to each other that ought to be exercised at the level of social organization closest to those in need. Individuals have responsibilities for themselves and families for their members. Neighbors have responsibilities for each other, exercised through both individual charity and voluntary organizations. The larger units of society—states and nations—have responsibilities for ensuring just structures and for caring for those who are not cared for at other levels. Catholic social teachings recognize that the taxing authority of the state and its coercive power are necessary to carry out these obligations.

On this issue as with the others analogues of the argument exist in secular philosophy. Utilitarians justify state action when the market fails. Liberals tend to assume that the state is a legitimate tool for collective action, since it is grounded in a social contract. Communitarians question both the utilitarian bias toward the market and the liberal bias toward the state, stressing instead individual and mutual responsibilities exercised in communities where people know and interact with each other. They criticize the welfare state for ignoring both personal responsibility for self-sufficiency and family obligations and for turning to the national government when intermediary institutions or the local government might be more appropriate. This communitarian concern, also shared by others, comes close to the Catholic notion of subsidiarity.

At this point, then, a policy analyst informed by Catholic teachings, whether or not they are framed in religious language, would conclude that all people have responsibilities to their communities; that communities have responsibilities to ensure opportunities for human flourishing to all their members; that fair treatment, care for the unfortunate, and the alleviation of deprivation are necessary; and that government can be an appropriate means for exercising such care, providing that the rights and responsibilities of lower levels of social organization are respected and met. Using these principles, I now move to more specific analyses of contemporary poverty and ways of dealing with it.

Contemporary U.S. Poverty and Policy

Poverty in the contemporary United States is a multifaceted phenomenon. Even when poverty is defined narrowly as material deprivation or low income, a look at the characteristics of those identified as poor suggests multiple underlying processes and, similarly, multiple possible policy approaches. Using U.S. Bureau of the Census data on the characteristics of the income poor in 2001, I identify three dimensions along which the poor are differentially distributed and use these dimensions to guide a discussion of policy alternatives:

—African Americans, Hispanics, and immigrants are disproportionately poor. African Americans make up about one-quarter of the income poor and Hispanics another quarter.

—The poor are about evenly divided between the working poor and their families and those who do not work. Nonworkers include both those who are not expected to work (elderly and disabled people) and those who cannot find or hold jobs or who choose not to work. Poverty rates among nonelderly nonworkers are extremely high.

—About one-quarter of the poor receive some form of means-tested cash assistance. Welfare recipients (families with children, headed for the most part by women, that receive TANF benefits) make up less than one-fifth of the poor.

The discussion illustrates the interplay among the different criteria and between values and empirical evidence and predictions. It also, I hope, illustrates that men and women of good will, including those who share a set of religious commitments, can arrive at different conclusions about specific policies, sometimes because they give different weights to important values and often because they have different interpretations of empirical facts and predictions. In most instances I prefer one approach or one policy conclusion over others and try to indicate whether the preference comes from a particular analytic approach, from an assessment of the empirical evidence, or from a judgment to err on one side or another in the context of uncertainty.

RACIAL JUSTICE AND HUMAN INVESTMENT POLICIES

Among the most troubling facts about poverty in the contemporary United States are the striking differences between the poverty rates of whites and African Americans and Hispanics in conventional measures of income poverty, wealth, employment, education, cognitive skills, incarceration, and mortality, among others. For example, in 2001 the income poverty rate for non-Hispanic whites was 7.8 percent, for African Americans 22.7 percent, and for Hispanics 21.4 percent. Life expectancy at birth in 2000 was seven years shorter for black males than for white males and five years shorter for black females than for white females. In 1997 black males were incarcerated at the rate of seven in one thousand, whereas the rate for white males was one in one thousand.[28]

The magnitude of these and other differences means that despite the fact that African Americans constitute only 13 percent of the U.S. population, they made up 16 percent of adults who did not work during the year 2000, 25 percent of the income poor in that year, and 42 percent of the incarcerated. Hispanics made up another 23 percent of the income poor. Addressing poverty requires, simply on the basis of numbers, addressing poverty among African Americans and Hispanics and therefore asking whether there is something distinctive about poverty in these groups that requires special policy attention. My analysis of this question relies heavily on Glenn Loury's *The Anatomy of Racial Inequality*.[29]

AFRICAN AMERICANS. Differences between native-born African Americans and whites have persisted over a long period of time. Explanations for these long-lasting racial differences in poverty rates and other measures of disadvantage tend to attribute the differences to one of three causes: discrimination, culture, or inherent differences in capacities. American public opinion by and large rejects the inherent capabilities explanation and also believes that overt discrimination has been largely eliminated by the civil rights laws of the last forty years. The cultural explanation takes note of higher rates of nonmarital pregnancy, crime, nonemployment, and school drop-out rates among African Americans, all of which are correlated with poverty, and hypothesizes that all are aspects of a destructive ghetto culture.

Loury argues, in contrast, that perceptions of inherent differences, which clearly shaped racial attitudes before emancipation, are structured in many ways into relationships between blacks and whites and in turn perpetuate racial inequality. Self-destructive behaviors on the part of some blacks are part of this pattern, but not uniquely causal.

At the foundation of Loury's argument is the axiom that there are no inherent differences in human capacities among racial groups. He justifies his assertion by noting that racial categories are social constructions with artificially drawn boundaries. A religious sensibility also would be inclined toward this axiom. The religious conception of human persons, which lies at the foundation of both Catholic social teaching and the Catholic sensibility, is that humanity has been created by God in God's image, that all humans are equally precious to God, and that all are brothers and sisters to each other. In God's eyes there are no important differences—"neither Jew nor Greek, slave nor free, male nor female."[30] Individual humans obviously vary enormously, along many dimensions, but the notion of equality in the sight of God suggests the assumption that no group of humans is inherently superior or inferior to any other.

This axiom leads Loury to the construction of an alternative explanation of racial differences, built on another assumption that also is fundamental to Catholic social teachings and the Catholic sensibility: that human persons are inherently social and are shaped by the human communities in which they live and develop. With these assumptions, Loury constructs an account of racial inequality based on notions of self-confirming racial stereotypes, conventions rooted in racial stigma, and development bias resulting from racial isolation.

Loury's first concept is that of self-confirming racial stereotypes, which arise because of the lack of information on which to make decisions. He gives a number of examples in which both blacks and whites behave rationally given the information they have but that result in a self-perpetuating vicious circle that harms blacks. A simple example is that of a cabdriver deciding whether to pick up a fare and balancing the potential gain from the fare against the risk of being robbed. The cabdriver knows from his own experience and that of his peers that the probability of robbery for any individual ride is very low but that the probability is higher if the fare is African American or is picked up in or driven to a poor African American neighborhood. He may rationally decide that the risk of picking up an African American outweighs the potential gain.

Meanwhile, African Americans, deciding whether to take cabs or to use alternative transportation, know from their own experience that they may well be unable to hail a cab. Many of them therefore decide not to bother, thus decreasing the number of law-abiding African Americans who hail taxicabs and thereby increasing the probability (still low) that any individual rider will be a robber. The self-confirming racial stereotypes lead to a situation in which law-abiding African Americans are disadvantaged, an outcome that also can occur in other interactions, for example, when they seek employment or credit.

But the cabdrivers also are disadvantaged, by missing fares. So why, Loury asks, do they not figure out that the information on which they are making decisions is faulty and look for more accurate ways to distinguish potential robbers from others? Loury argues that they do not bother to do this because the situation seems natural to them, not something that needs to be questioned. And this occurs, Loury argues, because of racial stigma that has over time been built into the ways in which blacks and whites interact with each other—what Loury calls racial conventions.

During the period of American slavery, whites developed ways of perceiving and dealing with blacks that legitimated the master-slave relationship—for example, by seeing blacks as not fully human. The racial conventions that arose out of this perception included reluctance on the part of whites, which persists to the present, to develop close egalitarian relationships with blacks. U.S. blacks and whites, by and large, do not marry each other and for the most part do not live in the same neighborhoods. This too can lead to vicious circles, resulting in persisting disadvantage for blacks. For example, whites perceive black inner-city neighborhoods as unattractive and dangerous places and treat their inhabitants with avoidance and fear. This can lead some inner-city residents to conclude that they have few good alternatives to lawless and self-destructive behavior. Thus what some label a culture of ghetto poverty is for Loury part of a vicious circle generated and perpetuated by racial stigma.

What Loury calls discrimination in contact—the avoidance of social relationships across races—also can lead to developmental disadvantages for blacks because they lack the cross-race and cross-class networks of relationships that are so important in the contemporary United States both for developing skills and for gaining access to opportunities. Even when blacks are able to obtain schooling equivalent to that of whites, discrepancies in their social capital inhibit advancement and sometimes reinforce destructive behavior. This in turn can perpetuate the behavior on the part of whites that keeps the disadvantaging racial conventions in place.

Loury thus argues that a profound historical injustice, chattel slavery, generated patterns of racial stigma that shaped interactions between blacks and whites and persist into the present because of self-reinforcing racial conventions. These patterns of interaction cannot be easily addressed by antidiscrimination laws, which largely and rightly govern contractual rather than intimate relationships. Loury argues that this analysis leads to a moral requirement for policies that address the persisting effects of the historical injustice, not through reparations but through policies that explicitly promote racial egalitarianism.

Logically, such policies could include those that favor blacks in their access to developmental opportunities that increase human capital: the education, skills, and behaviors that enhance productivity and lead to greater success in the labor market. Investments in education and health have long been central to antipoverty efforts, both in this country and in the developing world. Well-educated people do much better than those who are poorly educated, and the income and wealth gap between the two has been growing. Investments in education at all levels, from preschool to graduate school, have been shown to have important effects on income poverty as well as to enhance human flourishing by increasing cognitive capabilities.[31]

One could argue that in planning investments in education, health services, and economic opportunities, policymakers should look at their racial effects: for example, at the likely beneficiaries of a particular policy to reduce class size or to expand preschool education. Policies that have the effect of giving blacks an advantage would be justified and may be required. Strategies that locate health and educational services in black neighborhoods presumably would be similarly justified and would reinforce the importance of community as well as family and neighborhood responsibility.

Loury notes that the patterns he describes are mutually reinforcing and that some African Americans, especially in socially isolated inner-city neighborhoods, engage in antisocial and self-destructive behavior: crime, substance abuse, too early and nonmarital pregnancy, neglect of schooling, poor work habits, and so on. Loury explains these behaviors in the context of racial stigma and its effects, but he does not justify or excuse the behaviors. Presumably, although Loury does not say this, both parties in the self-reinforcing vicious circles are responsible for breaking them: in this case, whites are responsible for ensuring developmental opportunities; blacks, for taking advantage of them.

Loury's argument, it seems to me, is consistent with Catholic social teachings and is well expressed in religious language. His approach and perhaps even his conclusions may indeed be required by the fundamental assumptions of the teachings. Loury's arguments apply equally strongly to Native Americans, against whom terrible injustices were perpetrated. The power of the concepts and arguments may be tested, however, by seeing how well they apply to another important group among the poor, those of Hispanic origin.

HISPANICS AND IMMIGRANTS. The poverty rate in 2001 for those who identified themselves to the Census Bureau as being of Hispanic origin was 21.4 percent, and Hispanics made up 24 percent of the poor. Like African Americans, then, Hispanics make up a substantial proportion of the poor, raising questions about whether there is something particular to their circumstances that requires special policy attention, as with African Americans.

It is important to note that about one-third of the Hispanic poor in 2000 were immigrants and perhaps another third were native-born children of immigrants.[32] About 30 percent of the Hispanic poor were noncitizens. It is not possible to estimate the proportion of noncitizens who were undocumented rather than legal immigrants. The poverty rates in 2000 for immigrant and native-born Hispanics are about the same overall, but noncitizen immigrants have higher rates: 24 percent for foreign-born noncitizens, 21.1 percent for native-born Hispanics (including the citizen children of immigrants), and 13.2 percent for foreign-born citizens.

These facts raise important moral and policy questions about perceptions and treatment of immigrant compared with native-born Hispanics of different generations, of citizens compared with noncitizens, and of legal compared with undocumented immigrants. Should all or some of the Hispanic poor be granted the special attention that I argue is due blacks on the grounds of the historical injustice done to them? Conversely, are noncitizens or undocumented noncitizens appropriately dealt with less generously than citizens?

One question is whether treatment of native-born Hispanics, especially those who have been here for several generations, is analogous to that of African Americans in perpetuating racial stigma, self-confirming racial conventions of interaction, and developmental bias. It seems possible, indeed likely, that this would be the case for certain groups in certain places. Though Hispanics were never enslaved, Mexicans and some other Latin Americans, especially those with darker skins, were exploited by employers, with the exploitation perhaps defended, as slavery was, by the false notion that they were not fully and equally human. That could have set up the same kind of dynamic in interaction as that between whites and African Americans. On the other hand, what Loury calls discrimination in contact seems not to be nearly so prevalent against Hispanics as against blacks: intermarriage is much more common between Hispanics and whites, and the standard measures of residential segregation are much lower for Hispanics than for blacks. It would seem that the arguments for paying special policy attention to Hispanics are similar to those for African Americans, but not as strong.

Immigrants raise different questions. Following massive immigration to the United States over the last thirty years, 10 percent of the U.S. population was foreign born in 2000, with the percentage rising every year. About 20 percent of the poor in 1998 were members of immigrant households.[33] It seems clear that immigrants to the United States come of their own volition; indeed, the struggles that many endure to get here suggests that they very much want to come. They come in search of a better life, and despite their relatively high poverty rates it is clear that they are indeed better off than they would have been had they remained in their home countries. Immigrants are owed, of course, fair and nonexploitative treatment by employers and others, but the fact that they freely chose to come means that they are not owed in justice the compensatory treatment that is owed to blacks.

Of course, the question that preoccupies the public and Congress is not whether immigrants should receive preferential treatment but whether they should receive worse treatment. Undocumented immigrants are precluded from working legally and excluded from most government services and benefits. Legal immigrants who are not citizens had their access to welfare, food stamps, and other benefits severely limited by the welfare reform legislation of 1996. These policies were adopted in 1996 primarily as cost-saving provisions, but they were justified by the desire to deter immigrants who come to this country primarily or partly to receive benefits. There is also concern that large inflows of unskilled immigrants compete with African Americans for low-skill jobs and keep wages low in the labor markets in which they compete.[34]

It may well be that it is in the treatment of immigrants that Catholic social teachings and sensibilities have their most radical bite. The scriptural mandate to love your neighbor is not limited to the neighbor who looks like you, who lives near you, or who is a fellow citizen. The Hebrew Scriptures instruct us to welcome the alien and the stranger. The Christian Scriptures make clear that all are to be welcomed into the fellowship of Jesus and that our responsibilities extend to all of our fellow beings as brothers and sisters and children of God. In this context, it seems hard to justify raising barriers to entry or excluding some people from the resources of the society. It has, of course, long been accepted that nation states have the right to control their borders and to limit immigration. The moral justification for this is not clear to me, but immigration policy, thankfully, is beyond the scope of this volume. The deep commitment to human equality that underlies Loury's powerful analysis of racial inequality, however, certainly provides no excuse for discriminatory treatment of immigrants in policies designed to alleviate poverty.

GENERATING EMPLOYMENT

Work is both essential to human flourishing and tightly related to material and other aspects of well-being. Income poverty rates are higher among one-worker families than among two-worker families and much higher among families with no workers. In 2000 the poverty rate for members of families with no full-time workers was 30 percent (nonworking elderly families are included in the base); for members of families with one full-time worker the poverty rate was 10 percent; and for those in families with two or more full-time workers the poverty rate was 2 percent.

The differences in the size of the groups as well as the differences in poverty rates mean than in 2000 about 48 percent of the poor overall could be described as working poor and 52 percent as nonworking poor.[35] (About a fifth of the nonworking poor are elderly; another fifth are non-working poor adults who live alone; and the rest are members of families in which no one works full-time.) The working poor recently have received much-deserved policy attention. In the last fifteen years, federal social spending has shifted dramatically toward working poor families through a major expansion of the earned income tax credit (EITC) and through expansions of child care and health care for children.[36] The EITC, in contrast to other means-tested programs, is available only to working families and amounts to an income supplement of up to 40 percent of earned income. In 1990 federal spending on the means-tested TANF (Temporary Assistance for Needy Families) program was $23.6 billion; it was $9.6 billion on the EITC. By 1999 federal spending on TANF had decreased to $13.4 billion, while spending on EITC had increased to $31.9 billion. Many analysts and advocates, including

Catholic Charities USA, continue to push for expansion of these programs for the working poor—arguing, rightly, I believe, that for any families with a full-time worker to be poor is a matter of concern.

Here, however, I will focus on the nonworking poor, both because lack of work is so highly correlated with poverty and because work is in itself an important component of well-being. Unemployment—independent of income—is correlated with and probably contributes to other misfortunes, for example, depression and domestic abuse. Most people consider work itself to be a good: they want to be self-sufficient, to contribute to society, and to do something productive and useful with their time. The Christian tradition reinforces that intuition. Jesus' healings functioned explicitly to restore those cured to their place in the community, with new opportunities to participate and contribute. Paul bragged about the fact that he supported himself in his apostolate rather than relying on charity and urged others to do the same; he famously advised the Thessalonians that those who can work must do so if they want to eat.[37]

Market economies function well in creating jobs and matching those seeking employment with jobs. They signal the kinds of investments employment seekers should make and the activities they should undertake. Well-functioning capital markets provide financing for small investors as well as large, and they reward entrepreneurship and innovation. The number of employed persons (that is, the number of jobs) in the United States increased by 24 million between 1990 and 2000, while the labor force grew at the same rate and the official unemployment rate stayed relatively low.[38] In many developing countries, markets performed equally well, although the 1990s saw several instances in which the lack of appropriate regulation of markets and of an institutional foundation for them proved disastrous.

Labor markets do not work perfectly, however. Business cycles have not been eliminated. Unemployment rates vary regionally, with some neighborhoods, cities, and rural areas characterized by very high levels of joblessness. Some groups of people have much more trouble finding jobs than others, and some cannot find jobs that match their skills, their educational background, or their geographic location.

Nor do markets always generate economic rewards adequate to support a standard of living that permits full membership in the society. If we think, for example, that the poverty line represents a minimally adequate standard of living in this society and if we assume that a full-time worker typically supports one or two other people—for example, two workers, one full-time, for a family of four—then we would want full-time jobs held by working-age adults to pay between $11,239 and $13,738. Those are the poverty levels for families of two and three, respectively, equivalent to between $5.60 and $6.80 an hour. Instead, we see that about 8 percent of full-year full-time workers in 2000 earned below these levels.

Human investment strategies in education, health services, and job training offer one policy approach to providing opportunities for well-paying work. Their logic is that physically healthy, skilled, and educated people are more productive and more attractive to employers. Especially in our information-based economy, increasing levels of education and skill are necessary. In the developing world, primary health care and primary and secondary education are considered to be crucial to employment and development.

What else, if anything, is necessary to ensure opportunities for productive employment for all? One approach is based on the premise that labor markets work well and that most joblessness results from choosing not to work or from motivations and attitudes that get in the way of finding and holding a job. This approach emphasizes that alternatives to work—for example, welfare and unemployment benefits—should be short-term and unattractive in order to counteract some people's lack of motivation to work. It also may emphasize job preparation programs that focus on behaviors and attitudes like punctuality, pleasantness, and deference to supervisors.

An alternative approach is based on the premise that the market does not necessarily create jobs for everyone and that public intervention is appropriate and necessary to limit joblessness as much as possible, ideally to those who are between jobs and to those who genuinely have chosen not to work. Various tools are available for doing this. Macroeconomic management manipulates the money supply, interest rates, and level of government spending to affect the levels of unemployment and inflation and the trade-offs between them. During the 1990s in the United States, macroeconomic policies were able to maintain a level of unemployment that was considerably lower than most economists had believed was compatible with low inflation, a salutary achievement that required some risk taking on the part of the authorities but now is widely celebrated.

Much more controversial are policies to stimulate or actually create jobs. These policies can be of several sorts: for example, they may entail public service employment, wage subsidies, or local economic development projects.[39] One argument against such programs is that public job creation is inherently less efficient than private job creation and that it distorts the labor market. In making this argument, one can, of course, point to the well-documented failures of socialist states. The preference for market solutions to economic problems is now widespread, even among proponents of job creation. They tend to advocate that job creation programs should be relatively small scale, temporary, and targeted and that they should complement and support the private sector.

These limited programs are contested mainly on practical grounds. The question is not so much whether it would be desirable to create jobs as whether it is possible to do so at a reasonable cost. I approach this issue with a bias toward job creation; I assert, partly on the basis of my Catholic stance, both the importance of work and the failure of the market to provide jobs for all.

But my Catholic bias must confront the widespread perception that many of the direct job creation efforts tried so far have been wasteful and nonproductive and in some cases corrupt. The evidence is quite mixed. Some of the public service employment programs designed in the 1970s under the Comprehensive Employment and Training Act (CETA) deserved criticism. Some poorly designed wage subsidy programs actually decreased employment among their alleged beneficiaries by identifying them to employers as less productive workers. Job creation programs are costly—some of them very costly. Poorly designed programs have led to displacement of other workers, and they often are opposed by unions for that reason. And some programs in the public sector have led to increases in the size of government, which is opposed by many, in and of itself. All of this has led to political rejection of job creation approaches. Economic development efforts, like downtown redevelopment or enterprise/empowerment zones, have a more mixed record, but here too the empirical evidence is discouraging.

On the other hand, there is now considerable evidence that job creation programs can be implemented well, can have positive effects on those who participate, and can be cost effective. Bartik reviews all the studies and concludes, not surprisingly, that both design and implementation are crucial.[40] He is especially positive about targeted, short-term wage subsidy programs that encourage private and nonprofit employers to hire disadvantaged workers whose wage subsidies are supplemented by job training. His review also suggests that public service employment programs, run by government or under contract with nonprofits, can be effective with specific groups in specific places.

Another approach to economic development provides credit for small business development, including microcredit. This approach is very popular in developing countries as a strategy for making the informal sector of the economy more economically viable. In some situations this approach seems to have been successful; the example of the Grameen Bank in India is frequently cited.

It is less clear that microcredit strategies have much relevance for depressed economic areas in the United States. Reforming credit institutions so that they operate fairly and effectively for low-income people and allow those with entrepreneurial talents to start business ventures is a matter of simple fairness. But few of the poor in the United States have the necessary skills to enter our very competitive business climate, and the failure rates for small businesses are huge. Microcredit may well be a good thing, but it should not be considered a general strategy for alleviating poverty in this country.

Economic development and job creation programs are examples of policies for which empirical evidence on both feasibility and effectiveness is crucial. However good one's intentions, however desirable it might be to create jobs, if it cannot be done effectively and reasonably efficiently, it is not good policy. Hope is not a substitute for evidence. The existing evidence does not contradict the public's suspicion of large-scale general job creation. It does, however, suggest that well-designed targeted programs can work and that analysis and experimentation should continue.

INCOME TRANSFER POLICIES

Both secular and religious analysts of poverty prefer policies that create opportunities in the labor market to policies that simply transfer income. The Catholic tradition emphasizes people's responsibility to contribute to society and also emphasizes the value of participation and inclusion. In American society, being outside the labor market is exclusionary and stigmatizing. People aspire, and ought to aspire, to productive lives that contribute to their families and communities.

Nevertheless, there are times in people's lives when work is not a viable option, because of temporary or chronic disabilities, an economic downturn, or simply falling on hard times. There are children whose parents may not be able or may not choose to work but who clearly cannot work themselves. There are those who, in most developed countries, are not expected to work—for example, the elderly. The Christian tradition mandates generous, compassionate, and dignified care for those who cannot or are not expected to work. The Catholic tradition asserts that private charity, while laudable, must be supplemented when necessary by government intervention to provide such care. Income transfer policies are a key component of the care network.

Social insurance policies are part of this network. Old Age, Survivors, and Disability Insurance (Social Security) is the major social insurance program in the United States; others include workers' compensation and unemployment insurance. The principle here is that risk is distributed across the population and that benefits are related to contributions. Social Security has been a remarkable success in reducing poverty and enhancing life for the elderly, and it has wide political support. Current policy debates about Social Security reform raise some very interesting issues about the extent to which contributions rather than redistribution ought to determine benefits and about the relative effectiveness of public and private institutional mechanisms, but they will not be dealt with here. Nor will I deal with the serious shortcomings of the unemployment compensation system.

The largest means-tested income transfer program in the United States is now the earned income tax credit, which in 1999 distributed about $31.9 billion in federal funds to about 19.5 million recipients. The EITC, as noted above, is an earnings supplement available to low-income families with children in an amount of up to 40 percent of earnings to a maximum of about $4,000 for families earning between $10,000 and $12,000. The supplement phases out so that no benefits go to families with incomes above about $30,000.

The EITC is very popular politically, despite periodic concerns about possible fraud. Its popularity rests on the fact that it goes only to the working poor and provides no benefits to those who do not work. It also is well-targeted in that virtually all its benefits go to low-income families, unlike the minimum wage, most of the benefits of which go to secondary workers in nonpoor families. Morally, it has few drawbacks: it provides for the poor through legitimate collective action in a way that reinforces the obligations to support one's self and to take responsibility for one's family. Expansions of the EITC have been enthusiastically supported by Catholic lobbying groups.

The major policy controversies in recent years have revolved around two other means-tested assistance programs, the food stamp program and Temporary Assistance for Needy Families, formerly Aid to Families with Dependent Children (AFDC). The food stamp program spent about $15.5 billion in 2001, serving a monthly average of 17.3 million recipients. TANF spent about $12.5 billion on about 5.5 million recipients.

The food stamp program is the closest thing the United States has to a guaranteed minimum level of subsistence for everyone. Food stamps are vouchers (now delivered mostly through an electronic benefit system) that can be used for food purchases. A family of three is entitled to a maximum food stamp benefit of $356 a month, a family of four to $452 a month. Food stamp recipients are expected to spend 30 percent of their income after deductions on food; that amount is deducted from food stamp benefits. This structure means that individuals and families with incomes up to about the poverty line are eligible for some food stamp benefits.[41]

The food stamp program has been relatively popular politically, partly because it supports farmers as well as the poor. There are periodic debates over whether noncitizens should be eligible for food stamps (currently most are not) and whether there should be work requirements for nondisabled adults (currently there are, but they are very sporadically enforced). Food stamps represent a kind of uneasy moral compromise, a stingy good samaritanism. Support levels are low, the application process is complicated and discouraging, and the use of stamps (or the special electronic benefits card) visibly sets recipients apart. At the same time, food stamps symbolize a perhaps reluctant but nonetheless continuing societal commitment to the belief that people, however "unworthy," should not go hungry in this land of plenty. Therefore it would seem to be a matter for concern that according to official data, only 59 percent of those eligible for food stamps actually received them in 2000, down from a participation rate of 74 percent in 1994. Clearly people either do not know that they are eligible for food stamps or find the process of applying for them too demeaning or troublesome to bother with. This, I believe, is the current most pressing problem facing the food stamp program: to communicate effectively and to administer the program in a way that is humane and welcoming.

AFDC was instituted as part of the original Social Security Act to provide support in their own homes for children deprived of the support of a parent. At the time the image of a typical client was that of a widow who did not and was not expected to work and her children. The program continues to be used primarily by single-parent families with children. It provides modest cash grants and other services, with benefit levels and eligibility criteria largely determined by the states. In the median state, maximum monthly benefits for a family of three in 1996 were $415 per month.[42]

In 2000 a monthly average of 1.6 million adults and 4.4 million children received TANF grants. (Thirty-five percent of TANF cases were children only; that is, they included no adult recipients.) If we assume that all TANF recipients were poor, which is generally true, then TANF provided income assistance for only about one-fifth of the poor and only about 10 percent of poor nonelderly adults. Its actual importance and cost should not, therefore, be overestimated.[43]

Nonetheless, because TANF is the income transfer program that attracts the most public attention, its design and operation raise a number of important issues. One has to do with the relationship between cash assistance and work—the extent to which cash assistance of certain levels or types deters or fails to support work, which is valued in itself and not just for reasons of efficiency. A second has to do with the extent to which TANF encourages the formation of female-headed families or discourages marriage. A third concerns the locus of responsibility for determining and delivering assistance—the local, state, or national level. A fourth has to do with the character of the interaction between those who administer assistance programs and those who use them.

The last issue seems to me the easiest to comment on. The Catholic religious sensibility emphasizes the preciousness and dignity of every person and our mutual obligation to treat one another with respect and empathy. These qualities often are not characteristic of welfare administration. Sometimes welfare systems consciously choose to treat people badly, to deter their use of assistance; in other cases undignified treatment results from incompetence, lack of concern, or poor organizational design. In any case, a religious sensibility ought to challenge the welfare administration to design its procedures and conduct its interactions in a way that recognizes every person as a fully human child of God, with all the dignity that entails.

The issue of the locus of responsibility is more complicated, involving both the American notion of federalism and the Catholic notion of subsidiarity. The logic behind subsidiarity is that responsibility ought to be exercised and care provided at the most intimate level that is effective, by the units that are closest to poor families and by small communities. The preference is for kin networks, neighborhoods, and local voluntary organizations, the idea being that these groups know the individuals and the problems best and can tailor assistance and solutions effectively and compassionately. By the same logic, local government is preferred over state government, which is preferred over the federal government.

Sometimes forgotten in discussions of level of responsibility, however, is a qualification of the notion of subsidiarity: higher levels of civil society and government must take responsibility when lower levels cannot or do not. Neighbors provide care when families fail; local governments assume responsibilities not exercised by neighborhood groups; the federal government acts when state action is inadequate or inequitable.

The federalism question was a major focus of the debates over welfare reform in the mid 1990s.[44] Critics of the AFDC system in the form it took before 1996 claimed, with cause, that the federal government overregulated and stymied activities of the states. On the other side, advocates reflected on the gross historical disparities in states' treatment of the poor and especially of racial minorities and urged that federal guarantees and requirements be maintained.

The privatization question also was a focus of debate. Critics argued that government bureaucracies were not very good at delivering efficient and effective services and that they tended to be unresponsive and wasteful. Although there had been a long history of contracting out service provision to non-for-profit organizations, many wanted to expand contracting to both faith-based and profit-making organizations. There was little opposition to an important role for not-for-profit contractors, but questions were raised about the dangers of religious discrimination and religious proselytizing by faith-based service providers. Questions also were raised about the desirability of having profit-making firms perform such work as determining eligibility for benefits: were the incentives not likely to lead to cost savings at the expense of fair and compassionate treatment of applicants?

The 1996 welfare bill led to a dramatic devolution of power over the welfare system from the federal government to the states and also to an expansion of the power to enter contracts for services. The issues persist, however, in debates about welfare reauthorization, charitable choice, and the possibility of turning the food stamp program, for example, into a block grant program. On these issues, religious sensibilities can help frame the debates, but they can be only partially helpful in their resolution. The issues are of two types: one has to do with the relative importance of fair treatment, responsiveness, equity, and innovation. All these values are desirable, but the proper balance among them is not obvious. Empirical and predictive questions also are relevant to the discussion: How competent are state governments? To what extent have states overcome their histories of racism and discrimination? To what extent would state action compromise the legitimate expectation of American citizens for fair treatment?

My personal well-documented opposition to the 1996 welfare law rested partly on serious concerns about fair treatment by states and on the conviction that care for the poor is a national responsibility that ought to be shared by all.[45] Similar concerns lead me now to oppose proposals to block grant or devolve responsibility for the food stamp program. These judgments are based not on a rejection of the principle of subsidiarity but on the belief that the involvement of the higher level of government is necessary to ensure the fair and effective provision of assistance to the needy.

The question of family formation also is complicated. Many researchers have devoted much time and computing power to trying to determine whether the existence, level, or design of welfare benefits contributed to the dramatic increase in female-headed families and in nonmarital births between 1970 and 1990. The evidence is mixed. Female-headed family formation and nonmarital births went up over the same time that real welfare benefits went down. Most of the research suggests that factors other than welfare benefits were causal. Nonetheless, it is true that the very existence of welfare benefits makes it more possible for women to have and raise children independently. Welfare and, more important, the work opportunities now available to women make it less necessary for them to get married.

Catholic social teaching, American public opinion, and research all stress the desirability of raising children in a family headed by a married couple. It is important to look for and eliminate design features of the program (like limiting eligibility for benefits to female-headed families) that seem to discriminate against marriage. But there is no way to eliminate the fact that if we provide help to children in such families we make it more possible for them to exist. In my reckoning, the harm that would be done to children by eliminating or dramatically reducing cash assistance far outweighs any positive effect on family formation.

I do support strong child-support enforcement efforts as a way of enforcing parental responsibility and discouraging pregnancy in casual sexual liaisons. I am not opposed to experimental programs to encourage marriage or keep marriages together, as long as they do not divert substantial resources from other uses; I have seen little convincing evidence that such programs are effective, but perhaps some can be designed. On this issue, I believe that some small undesirable consequences simply have to be lived with, in the service of compassion toward and care for needy children.

The issue of work incentives and requirements in cash assistance programs also is very complicated. The Christian sensibility ought to be compassionate and hopeful; it ought to want to be generous toward those in need, especially those who are victims of circumstances, and it ought to give others the benefit of the doubt—assuming until proven otherwise, for example, that a person would work if he or she could. But the Christian sensibility also values responsibility and participation; it values work. So a Christian approach would presumably be generous to those who could not work, temporarily or chronically, but it would focus on setting expectations and providing opportunities for those who can work to do so.

So what does this dual emphasis imply about work incentives, work requirements, and time limits in welfare programs? An argument can be made that work requirements in welfare programs are not necessary: that welfare benefits are sufficiently low, even in the most generous states, and that the system itself is sufficiently stigmatizing to ensure that people who can work will choose to do so, as long as working does not entail economic loss. All that is needed is to structure welfare benefits so that one always improves one's lot by working; requirements then will not be necessary. Welfare benefits can be relatively generous, as long as they are lower than what someone would earn at, say, a full-time minimum wage job.

Unfortunately, while this argument may be logical in theory, it did not seem to hold in practice before the welfare reforms of 1996. Benefit levels that are high enough to provide minimal nutrition and housing for a family are also high enough to make work unattractive, especially when welfare benefits are reduced by nearly a dollar for a dollar of earnings. For example, the median welfare plus food stamp benefit in 1999 was $664 per month. Even though full-time work at the minimum wage would have generated $875, work also means increased costs, for example, for child care and transportation; the risk of loss of health care benefits; and greatly reduced time for family and personal activities. Before the expansion of the earned income tax credit in the mid 1990s, moving from welfare to a full-time minimum wage job netted a single mother only $2,325 a year in net financial gain. (By 1999, with an expanded EITC and increased child care subsidies, the net financial gain was $7,051.)[46] In the absence of work requirements, benefits also can be supplemented by informal work, which technically must be reported and deducted from benefits but often is not.

Perhaps more important, whereas society once considered it unnecessary and indeed inappropriate for mothers, whether single or married, to work, large numbers of mothers now participate in the labor market. Much of the public considers it unfair to allow some people who could work to receive benefits while not working while in other families both parents work and struggle to support themselves without the help of the government.

There is another argument about work requirements that, along with the fairness argument, has led me to support them. It is an argument voiced by many welfare recipients themselves: that they needed the push of a work requirement to overcome their own lack of initiative in finding jobs or training experiences that later turned out to be valuable to them. This is not a unique failing on their part; many of us need the force of laws or requirements to do things that we know we should do. Requirements to participate in work or training can be a productive push that recipients later are grateful for.

Both historical and program evaluation evidence suggest that a combination of strategies that require participation in work or employment services and policies that reward work can result in both increased employment and increased family income. Between 1994 and 2000, welfare rolls dropped dramatically, employment of single mothers increased, and poverty rates for female-headed families dropped. During the same period, overall unemployment rates dropped as the economy boomed, the EITC expanded so that the rewards to work increased substantially, and welfare reform imposed work requirements and time limits. Analysts believe that all three factors were important in contributing to the results, probably in the order mentioned.[47]

The notion that work requirements combined with rewards for work enhance work and family well-being is supported by research done by the MDRC on two innovative programs, the Minnesota Family Assistance Program and the Canadian Self-Sufficiency Program.[48] Both programs existed in two versions, one that provided earnings supplements only and one that combined earnings supplements with participation in employment services, which in Minnesota was required. Both programs resulted in increased employment and earnings, with the Minnesota combined program proving especially effective.

What I have just articulated, of course, are arguments about work requirements in general, not about whether work requirements should be for twenty, thirty, or forty hours a week or about whether education and training can count for all or part of the requirement. In making these decisions, I believe that it is important to understand the characteristics of those who would be affected: their family responsibilities; their own disabilities and other barriers to work; their ability to benefit from various types of experiences. Reasonableness and compassion preclude, I believe, a forty-hour work requirement for parents of young children, especially those who, like many now remaining on the caseload, often are burdened by multiple problems. A Christian sensibility, as I have noted, balances important values; the trick is recognizing when the balance turns.

Time limits raise similar issues. The basic argument for time limits is that they send a strong message that welfare is temporary and that recipients are expected to move quickly to self-support. The argument against them is that they can be inappropriate and nonresponsive in individual situations and that they can leave vulnerable people, especially children, at risk. To some extent questions about time limits are empirical: Are they necessary to send a message of seriousness? Are they implemented with respect for individual situations and in recognition of the serious difficulties that people sometimes face in finding jobs? Are there provisions for care of the vulnerable after time limits expire? The 1996 welfare reform law imposed a five-year time limit on the receipt of federal welfare benefits. Because the implementation date of the law was 1997, evidence is not yet in on many of these questions. In deciding on exemptions to time limits and the formulation of any extension of time limits, all of this must be weighed.

In Conclusion

The modestly left-of-center policy conclusions on racial justice, job creation, and income transfers that I have reached in this chapter could perhaps have been predicted from my political history, independent of my faith. I have run large social service agencies, an activity that can make one both practical and humble, for both Bill Clinton and Mario Cuomo, which defines me as a Democrat. To this analysis, as to that work, I have brought my practical experience and my knowledge of social science, but I have brought also moral principles that for me have their roots in Catholic social teaching and in a Catholic sensibility that is shaped every day by prayer and worship.

I would like to think that the defining features of a Catholic approach to social policy are its empathy for all of God's people, especially the poor; its generosity; and its hopefulness. I would like to think that generosity and hopefulness characterize its arguments and approach to dialogue, as well as its prescriptions for spending our own and other people's money. In that spirit, I find many of my judgments tentative, more a matter of taking a chance in one direction or another than of proceeding confidently on the basis of empirical claims and moral logic.

I look forward to the dialogue.

Notes

1. This quote is from *Holy Bible: Today's New International Version: New Testament* (Grand Rapids, Mich.: Zondervan Publishers, 2002). In general, my scriptural citations will be from the New Revised Standard Version.

2. A disclaimer is no doubt in order right at the beginning. I am a social scientist and policy analyst by training and profession but an extremely amateur student of theology. I have read and consulted widely on my theological statements, but they should be taken as those of an informed lay person, not a professional. I am a practicing Catholic, active in my Dorchester parish.

3. A classic statement of the policy analytic framework is found in Edith Stokey and Richard Zeckhauser, *A Primer for Policy Analysis* (W.W. Norton and Company, 1978). A more recent statement is in Eugene Bardach, *A Practical Guide for Policy Analysis: The Eightfold Path to More Effective Problem Solving* (New York: Chatham House Publishers, 2000).

4. An excellent explanation of the nature of the teaching office is found in Francis A. Sullivan, *Magisterium: The Teaching Authority in the Catholic Church* (Mahwah, N.J.: Paulist Press, 1983).

5. Infallible teaching on faith and morals must be identified as such and is very rare. Very few papal teachings are clearly meant to be infallible; the clearest examples are those of the Immaculate Conception and the Assumption of Mary.

6. A comprehensive collection of the documents that make up Catholic social teachings is in David J. O'Brien and Thomas A. Shannon, eds., *Catholic Social Thought: The Documentary Heritage* (Maryknoll, N.Y.: Orbis Books, 1998).

7. National Conference of Catholic Bishops, *Economic Justice for All: Pastoral Letter on Catholic Social Teaching and the U.S. Economy* (Washington: 1986).

8. The bishops' letter on the economy is an interesting mix of what I call social teachings and their application to specific policy questions. The first half of the letter is a theological and ethical presentation, which the bishops mean to be authoritative. The second half is an application of the principles to specific policy questions

current in the mid 1980s, which the bishops recognize as dependent on empirical analysis and open to legitimate disagreement.

9. These ideas were most recently developed by John Paul II, Centesimus Annus: *On the Hundredth Anniversary of* Rerum Novarum. O'Brien and Shannon, eds., *Catholic Social Thought*, pp. 439–88.

10. Some of these reactions are found in R. Bruce Douglass, ed., *The Deeper Meaning of Economic Life: Critical Essays on the U.S. Catholic Bishops' Pastoral Letter on the Economy* (Georgetown University Press, 1986).

11. Novak has been especially critical of the bishops' 1988 letter on the economy and especially enthusiastic about John Paul II's Centesimus Annus. See Michael Novak, *The Catholic Ethic and the Spirit of Capitalism* (New York: Free Press, 1993). The theology of these two documents is, in my reading, quite consistent. Their policy conclusions on the desirability of a government "welfare state" are somewhat different.

12. Andrew M. Greeley, *The Catholic Myth: The Behavior and Beliefs of American Catholics* (Charles Scribner's Sons, 1990).

13. This definition and most statistics on income poverty in the United States come from U.S. Census Bureau, *Poverty in the United States*, Current Population Reports, P60-219, Government Printing Office, 2002 and from the more detailed table from the same survey that the Census Bureau makes available at http://ferret. bls.census.gov/macro/032002/pov/toc.htm [March 18, 2003]).

14. Amartya Sen, *Development as Freedom* (New York: Anchor Books, 1999), p. 3.

15. Ibid, p. 87.

16. Ibid, p. 36.

17. The UNDP approach and data on the human development indexes for all countries are described in its annual *Human Development Report*, the most relevant of which is United Nations Development Program, *Human Development Report 1997* (Oxford University Press, 1997), which focuses specifically on poverty.

18. The scriptural bases of Catholic social teaching are well explained in National Conference of Catholic Bishops, *Economic Justice for All*, chapter 2, part A. It references the relevant scriptural texts, which permits me to avoid scriptural citations. My own reading of Scripture is influenced also by various commentaries, one of the most important of which for me has been William Reiser, *Jesus in Solidarity with His People: A Theologian Looks at Mark* (Collegeville, Minn.: Liturgical Press, 2000).

19. John Paul II, *Centesimus Annus*.

20. John Rawls, *A Theory of Justice* (Harvard University Press, 1971).

21. Examples of the communitarian perspective are Michael J. Sandel, *Democracy's Discontent: America in Search of a Public Philosophy* (Harvard University Press, 1996); Philip Selznick, *The Moral Commonwealth: Social Theory and the Promise of Community* (University of California Press, 1994); and Selznick, *The Communitarian Persuasion* (Washington: Woodrow Wilson Center Press, 2002).

22. This concept is explored in Donal Dorr, *Option for the Poor: A Hundred Years of Catholic Social Teaching* (Maryknoll, N.Y.: Orbis Books, 1992).

23. Luke 18:18–27.

24. The most radical working out of the utilitarian perspective is that of Peter Singer. See, for example, "Famine, Affluence and Morality," in Peter Singer, *Writings on an Ethical Life* (HarperCollins, 2000).

25. Rawls, *A Theory of Justice*.

26. John Paul II, *Centesimus Annus*.

27. National Conference of Catholic Bishops, *Faithful Citizenship: Civic Responsibility for a New Millennium* (Washington, 1999).

28. Income poverty statistics are from U.S. Census Bureau, *Poverty in the United States: 2000*, Current Population Reports, P60-214 (Government Printing Office, 2001). Other statistics and many of the concepts used in the analysis are from Glenn C. Loury, *The Anatomy of Racial Inequality* (Harvard University Press).

29. Ibid.

30. Galatians 3:28.

31. Lynn A. Karoly, "Investing in the Future: Reducing Poverty through Human Capital Investments," in Sheldon H. Danzinger and Robert H. Haveman, eds., *Understanding Poverty* (Russell Sage Foundation and Harvard University Press, 2001), pp. 314–56, is an excellent review of the literature on human capital policies.

32. I made these estimates from data in *Poverty in the United States: 2000*, and *Profile of the Foreign-Born Population in the United States: 2000*, Current Population Reports, P23-206 (Government Printing Office, 2001).

33. Gary Burtless and Timothy M. Smeeding, "The Level, Trend, and Composition of Poverty," in Danzinger and Haveman, eds., *Understanding Poverty*, p. 58.

34. For analysis of the effects of immigration on African Americans, see the chapters in Daniel S. Hamermesh and Frank D. Bean, eds., *Help or Hindrance? The Economic Implications of Immigration for African Americans* (Russell Sage Foundation, 1998).

35. These calculations add together the poor in families, poor unrelated individuals from eighteen to sixty-four years of age, and poor elderly unrelated individuals, who I assumed were nonworkers. The data come from the U.S. Census Bureau (www.census.gov/hhes/www/poverty00.html [March 20, 2003]).

36. These policy trends are well documented and explained in John Karl Scholz and Kara Levine, "The Evolution of Income Support Policy in Recent Decades," in Danzinger and Haveman, eds., *Understanding Poverty*, pp. 193–228.

37. 2 Thessalonians 3:10.

38. Labor market and employment statistics come from the Department of Labor's Bureau of Labor Statistics (www.bls.gov [March 20, 2003]).

39. Timothy J. Bartik, *Jobs for the Poor: Can Labor Demand Policies Help?* (Russell Sage Foundation, 2001) is a comprehensive review of labor demand policies.

40. Ibid.

41. Information on the food stamp program and data on beneficiaries, spending, and participation are available through the U.S. Department of Agriculture (www.fns.usda.gov [March 20, 2003]).

42. LaDonna A. Pavetti, "Welfare Policy in Transition: Redefining the Social Contract for Poor Citizen Families with Children and for Immigrants," in Danzinger and Haveman, eds., *Understanding Poverty*, pp. 229–77, has an excellent description of the TANF program after the 1996 welfare reform, with good data on state variations.

43. TANF data from the Administration for Children and Families, U.S. Department of Health and Human Services (www.acf.dhhs.gov [March 20, 2003]).

44. The history and politics of welfare reform in the 1990s are well described in R. Kent Weaver, *Ending Welfare as We Know It* (Brookings, 2000). The effects of welfare reform and recommendations for the future are the subject of the excellent papers in Rebecca Blank and Ron Haskins, eds., *The New World of Welfare* (Brookings, 2001).

45. From 1993 to 1996, I was assistant secretary for children and families in the Department of Health and Human Services. I resigned that position after the president signed the welfare reform bill, along with Peter Edelman and Wendell Primus; the three of us felt the need to make a clear statement of our positions.

46. These calculations were done by my colleague David Ellwood.

47. See Blank and Haskins, *New World of Welfare*, for good reviews of the evidence.

48. Their results are reported in Dan Bloom and Charles Michalopoulos, *How Welfare and Work Policies Affect Employment and Income: A Synthesis of Research* (New York: MDRC, 2001).

A BIBLICAL RESPONSE
TO POVERTY

LAWRENCE M. MEAD

W HAT DOES THE Bible suggest that government should do about poverty? It is not a question that policy experts usually ask. In fact, participants in debates about poverty often speak out of religious conviction, either their own or what they believe other people's to be. But they seldom say explicitly what the norms should be. Venturing in where angels fear to tread, I dare to do that here.[1]

The subject is more important than it may appear. Keynes remarked that economic policy was often in thrall to "some defunct economist." Theologians who address poverty believe that they are powerless, in my experience. They say government ignores them. But church teachings about social ethics shape what society thinks "doing good" for the poor means. Like the poets Shelley spoke of, theologians are among the "unacknowledged legislators of mankind."

I write here as a Protestant, and I rely mainly on the New Testament gospels.[2] However, I know the secular literature about poverty and welfare far better than I know theological reflections on these subjects. In characterizing what churches say, I rely heavily on Catholic sources, because to me those were the most coherent and accessible. To a lesser extent, I rely on statements by several mainline denominations on welfare reform in congressional hearings. These statements suggest that Catholic and Protestant positions have been similar, although I cannot prove this.

I speak mainly about poverty in the United States and, by extension, other western countries. Poverty outside the West is quite different. I also discuss U.S. poverty mainly in the context of welfare reform, because that effort brings out the issues most sharply. "Welfare reform" here means the struggle, going back to the 1960s, to overhaul Aid to Families with Dependent Children (AFDC), the nation's controversial aid program for needy single-parent families. Congress revamped AFDC and renamed it Temporary Assistance for Needy Families (TANF) in the Personal Responsibility and Work Opportunity Reconciliation Act (PRWORA) of 1996.

I address several classic questions about the relationship between religion and social policy. Is there a duty to care for the poor? How is that responsibility distributed among poor people themselves, more fortunate people acting privately, and private and public sector institutions? How does a "religious" approach to poverty differ from a secular one? What does a religious assessment suggest about our current welfare policy and the reauthorization of TANF, which Congress is now considering?

I find it easy to say that there is a duty to the poor and that the onus of fulfilling that duty lies on the government and society as well as the individual. While a nonreligious approach to poverty is imaginable, it has little practical importance because approaches based on religious values are so dominant.[3] In American politics, even those who appear harsh toward the needy rationalize their stance in terms of values that are broadly biblical. Framed this way, none of these choices seems very difficult.

The contentious question in American social policy has more to do with the *character* of our response. Especially, can we demand anything from the poor in return for aiding them? That is different from the question of whether we should aid them at all. While many will say that individuals should help themselves before turning to government, the idea of forcing recipients to work as a condition of aid is still sensitive. That is what government is now doing, and the effects appear mostly favorable. Yet the policy was resisted by many experts and by most churches that I know of, speaking as organizations. The opponents act out of values that could be called religious, but so do the proponents. This is the issue, above all, that I probe below.

In addressing poverty, government is now ahead of the churches. Twenty years ago, the main division over poverty was between liberals or

Democrats who wanted to do more for the poor and conservatives or Republicans who wanted to do less. Both sides wished poor adults would work more regularly, but the left wanted to promote that goal with new incentives or training programs, the right by cutting back aid so that poor families would have no alternative to working. In the end, Congress chiefly changed the *character* rather than the *extent* of government effort. It made work a condition of receiving welfare.[4]

The theological debate has not caught up. For the most part, church officials still discuss the extent of public commitment to the poor rather than its nature. In Christian thought, there have always been schools that advocated public effort to help the poor, such as the social gospel of a century ago or liberation theology today. Other beliefs construe faith as a personal relationship with God and downplay social action, a stance favored by today's religious right. Neither side seriously contemplates the idea of requiring the poor to work *alongside* government, although that works best. Just as the political world needed a more civic form of conservatism, so theologians need a more civic conception of what helping the poor means.

My chief differences are with what I will call the institutional church. I mean by this the United States Catholic Conference and other church organizations that have taken public positions on poverty or welfare reform in the United States. These are not the whole of the church or even of its leadership, and their views are questioned by much of the laity. They have been the most permissive voices in the welfare debate, although they have become more moderate recently. Traditionally, they told government to do the most for the poor while demanding the least from them. I question that position, on both theological and practical grounds.

In what follows, I set out three premises to guide my assessment of antipoverty policy. I then use them to appraise the three chief positions that politically active people have taken toward that policy—to give aid by entitlement, without behavioral conditions; to reduce aid; and to link aid to work requirements. The last, I argue, is most in keeping with the Bible as well as the most effective. I close with some comments on TANF and its pending reauthorization.

Premises

Our response to poverty should be guided by how we understand the problem, what the Bible suggests that we should do about it, and the specific limitations of government.

WHAT IS POVERTY?

The empirical basis of this analysis is the character of poverty. What is it, and what are its causes? In the popular mind, to judge from U.S. opinion polls, being poor means having unusually low income for the society. It may also suggest that poor people have lost control of their lives. The poor then are those who are destitute by community standards *and* who may have done something to make themselves poor, such as failing to work or having children out of wedlock.[5] Poverty, therefore, raises questions of economic need alongside questions of "deservingness."

Poverty tends to be a concern mainly in affluent societies. Only there is destitution rare enough that it becomes objectionable and controversial, and only these societies are rich enough to do something about it. Western commentators—including church leaders—speak of poverty in developing countries too, but there low income as such is usually not an issue. These countries can do little to succor the destitute, although they may try. Poverty is still seen as part of the human condition. In the West, it is seen as an embarrassment that government must remove.

THE OFFICIAL POOR. In the United States, poverty is usually defined as it has been by the federal government since 1964. A minimum income is calculated based on three times the amount of money that families need just for food, and people who fall under that line are defined as poor. The poverty threshold varies with the size of family and is indexed for inflation. In 2001 the poverty line for a single person under age sixty-five was $9,214, while for a three-person family including two children under age eighteen it was $14,269. In 2001, 11.7 percent of Americans were poor; the rate has varied from 11 to 15 percent since 1970.[6]

Some argue that the federal poverty line is too low because today the cost of food has become much less than one-third of a minimal budget and because the official definition makes no allowance for higher living costs in urban areas, among other problems. Others argue that poverty is overestimated because in calculating income, only money sources such as earnings and public cash benefits are counted, not tax credits and in-kind benefits such as food stamps and Medicaid. With adjustments for such factors, the impoverished population might be somewhat larger or smaller than now calculated. But most experts accept the federal definition as meaningful for research purposes and for showing trends over time.

How often the poor by this definition suffer active hardship is unclear. On one hand, most middle-class people cannot imagine supporting a family on a poverty-level income. Living at that level, people assume, must be abusive. For some poor it undoubtedly is, especially for those living well below the poverty line. On the other hand, only a small proportion of the poor appear to suffer acute distress, such as hunger or homelessness. The federal poverty line, of course, is much higher than the incomes of $1 or $2 per person per day used to measure poverty in the developing world.

Surveys suggest that most families that are counted as poor consume at a level well above what they can apparently afford. That may be because they underreport their income. While we think of the poor as possessing no assets or amenities, in 1995–97, 41 percent of poor households owned their homes and majorities owned automobiles, color televisions, microwave ovens, and air conditioners. Inability to obtain food or medical care is rare among the poor, although not unknown. The material conditions faced by children at the bottom of society have probably improved in the last thirty years, despite family income trends that might suggest the opposite.[7]

The federal definition of poverty is entirely economic. Controversy about poverty is driven, however, largely by the "deservingness" issues. The worthy poor are those who appear to have become poor through no fault of their own, because of injury, age, or misfortune. Society helps support them with little dispute. The "undeserving" are those who seem to have got themselves into trouble; they include unwed mothers and the nonworking men who often father their children. Welfare is the most unpopular antipoverty program because it supports these latter groups, directly or indirectly. Poor children, of course, are innocent and deserving, but it is difficult to aid them without supporting their less popular parents. Whether the parents are in fact responsible for their predicament is the great question. While there are other poor people, I concentrate here on the working-age poor and welfare recipients, especially the long-term poor, simply because that is where the debate about poverty has centered.

Table 1 shows the distribution of the official poor across several social categories in 2001. While the poor are diverse, the incidence of poverty runs highest among children, racial minorities, female-headed families, and unrelated individuals (those outside families) and in central cities. All these groups are overrepresented among the poor relative to their share of the population. Above all, poverty is concentrated among female-headed families in the inner city—the same group that is at the core of the welfare debate.

If we consider those who have been poor for several years rather than one year, the preponderance of these groups is still greater. Over the period 1979–91, only 2 percent of whites were poor for ten years or more, while 17 percent of blacks were. Over 1974–87, only 6 percent of non-black families were on welfare for more than seven years at a stretch, but 25 percent of black families were. An earlier analysis found that in families that were poor for eight or more years during 1969–78, 44 percent of the family heads were nonelderly women and 62 percent were black; for families on welfare (mostly well below poverty) for eight or more years, the comparable figures were 58 and 55 percent.[8] Much of the sensitivity surrounding poverty derives from these ties to race and gender. Exactly how those demographic features help to cause poverty or dependency is, of course, disputed.

THE CAUSES OF POVERTY. Many people experience poverty, but usually only briefly. In 1979–91, one-third of Americans were poor for at least one year, but only 5 percent were poor for ten or more years.[9] Episodic poverty has many causes—illness, job loss, the breakup of a marriage. But transient poverty usually does not isolate people from the rest of society, and so it gets little attention. The more serious debate is over poverty that lasts for two or more years at a stretch.

Of the long-term poor, the elderly or disabled are not expected to work. Whether they are poor mainly reflects the adequacy of public benefits. In recent decades, the poverty rates for these groups fell sharply, mainly because of increased benefits paid by Social Security and disability programs. For the working-age poor, the causes of sustained poverty

TABLE I. *Poverty in the United States, 2001*[a]

Group	Number in group (millions)	Number of poor (millions)	Percent of group poor	Percent of people from group	Percent of poor from group
All persons	281	33	11.7	100	100
Male	138	14	10.4	49	44
Female	144	19	12.9	51	56
White	230	23	9.9	82	69
Black	36	8	22.7	13	25
Hispanic	37	8	21.4	13	24
Under age 18	72	12	16.3	26	36
Age 18–64	176	18	10.1	62	54
Age 65 and over	34	3	10.1	12	10
In metro areas	229	25	11.1	81	77
Central cities	81	13	16.5	29	41
Suburbs	148	12	8.2	52	37
In nonmetro areas	53	7	14.2	19	23
Northeast	53	6	10.7	19	17
Midwest	64	6	9.4	23	18
South	100	14	13.5	36	41
West	64	8	12.1	23	24
In families	234	23	9.9	83	71
Two-parent	182	10	5.7	65	31
Female-headed	39	11	28.6	14	34
Unrelated individuals	46	9	19.9	16	28
On means-tested aid	70	22	31.6	25	67
On food stamps	18	11	62.2	6	34

Source: U.S. Census Bureau, March 2002 Annual Demographic Supplement, tables 2–4.

a. Some figures do not add due to rounding. Races add to more than total because of double counting (Hispanics may be of any race). Families and unrelated individuals add to less than total because unrelated subfamilies are omitted. Family types add to less than total because male-headed single-parent families are omitted.

are more controversial. How is it possible for families to remain poor for many years in the United States, the world's richest country? I concentrate here on evidence apart from that arising from recent welfare reform, which I discuss later.

Long-term poor families tend to become poor because of the behaviors that make poverty controversial: Women have children out of wedlock, and then they or their spouses do not work regularly to support their children. Of the two causes, unwed pregnancy appears to be the less important, contrary to common opinion. Families become poor or go on welfare mainly because they lack earnings, not because they are headed by a woman, and that is especially true for the black poor.[10] Employment problems also help to produce female-headed families, in that failure to provide for their families causes many low-income men to abandon them—or to be driven out by their spouses.

The percentage of poor family heads who worked fell during the 1960s and early 1970s, in part because poverty was falling in those years. Rising real wages lifted most of the working poor above the poverty line, leaving a smaller and largely nonworking poor population behind. In the 1990s the number of working poor started to rise again, due largely, I will argue, to welfare reform. But the incidence of employment among poor adults is still strikingly low.

Table 2 contrasts employment status among the general population and the poor for persons age sixteen and over in 2001. While 69 percent of all adults worked at some time in the year, only 38 percent of poor adults did. More significant, 46 percent of the population worked full-time for the full year, compared with only 12 percent of the poor. That multiple of almost four times largely explains why most Americans avoid poverty and many poor do not. For family heads, the gap in overall work levels between the general population and the poor was not as great, but still, almost three times as many from the general population worked full-time full-year as those who were poor. Notably, female-headedness by itself does not explain low work levels. Among both the general population and the poor, female family heads have work levels quite similar to those of all family heads. In families with children, work levels for female heads are quite close to those for all heads. Much more important is the large difference in work levels between poor and nonpoor.

These figures do not establish how many more poor adults could work. In 2001, 28 percent of nonworking poor adults claimed to be ill or disabled, 26 percent retired, 22 percent at home for family reasons, and 20 percent in school; only 4 percent were unable to find work.[11] But since many people facing those conditions also work, the importance of the

TABLE 2. *Percent of Persons Age Sixteen and Older and Family Heads Who Worked, by Employment Status and Income Level, 2001*[a]

Employment status	Persons	All heads	Female Heads	With children under 18	
				All heads	Female heads
All income levels					
Worked at any time	69	75	73	86	80
Worked a full year, full-time	46	55	48	64	52
Did not work	31	25	27	14	20
Income below poverty line					
Worked at any time	38	51	54	60	58
Worked a full year, full-time	12	19	16	23	17
Did not work	62	49	46	40	42

Source: U.S. Census Bureau, March 2002 Annual Demographic Supplement, tables 10 and 17.

a. "Full year" means at least fifty weeks a year, "full-time" at least thirty-five hours a week.

impediments is difficult to assess. Government disability programs appraise applicants carefully before certifying them as unemployable.

These differing work rates have powerful effects on poverty. Table 3 shows poverty levels in 2001 for the same work and demographic categories used in Table 2. The levels are dramatically lower for the employed than the nonemployed. For people working full-time full-year, the poverty rate was mostly in the single digits, while for nonworking females with children, it reached 70 percent. That rate is not surprising, since under current policy, working-age people get little support other than from earnings. Admittedly, this table does not consider other factors that affect poverty besides employment, such as wage levels.

The importance of employment to poverty sometimes has been overlooked because of the belief that most of the poor are children or the elderly, groups that are not expected to work. That is no longer true. In 1959, 44 percent of the poor indeed were children and 14 percent were elderly, leaving 42 percent working age (ages eighteen to sixty-four). By 2001, however, the proportions had shifted to only 36 percent children,

TABLE 3. *Percent of Poor Persons Age Sixteen and Older and Poor Family Heads Who Worked, by Employment Status, 2001*[a]

				With children under 18	
Employment status	Persons	*All heads*	*Female Heads*	*All heads*	*Female heads*
All work levels	10	9	26	13	34
Worked at any time	6	6	20	9	25
Worked a full year, full-time	3	3	9	5	11
Did not work	21	18	44	37	70

Source: U.S. Census Bureau, March 2002 Annual Demographic Supplement, tables 10 and 17.
a. "Full year" means at least fifty weeks a year, "full-time" at least thirty-five hours a week.

10 percent elderly, and 54 percent working age.[12] The change reflects smaller families and the lifting of most of the elderly above the poverty level by Social Security. It also may reflect growing problems among low-skill adults at the bottom of society. So today, working-age adults and their children constitute a clear majority of the poor. That makes the work and family problems of the adults even more central to poverty than they were earlier.

Today, poverty among working-age adults also is closely tied to unwed childbearing. In 2001 only 18 percent of all family heads in the general population were single mothers, but among poor family heads the figure was 51 percent. In the AFDC program in 1996, the mothers of 60 percent of the children were unwed and the mothers of 25 percent were divorced or separated.[13] Problems with crime, substance abuse, and performance in school also are unusually prevalent among the poor, although far from unknown among the better-off.

—*Economic barriers.* But if not working and having children out of wedlock are the chief causes of poverty, that just pushes the question back: What causes those behaviors? The work problem has sparked the most intense research. Why, many scholars ask, do long-term poor adults not work more regularly? To a large extent, the debate over poverty is a debate about nonwork. While answers are elusive, it is clear that attributing the problem to impersonal social structures has become implausible.

Theologians usually adopt what I call a social democratic interpretation of poverty. They see it as due to "unemployment," by which they° mean a lack of jobs for willing workers.[14] Insufficient employment, in turn, is the great evil of capitalism, which generates jobs only to make a profit and not to employ the entire labor force. This view reflects critiques of the industrial economy going back to Marx and before. It is the main basis of papal encyclicals on poverty, from Leo XIII's *Rerum Novarum* of 1891 down to the statements of John Paul II, the current pope.[15] It also shaped the thought of Protestant critics of capitalism.[16]

In the social democratic theory, poverty is identified with the predicament of the traditional working class. Working-age adults are presumed to seek work and to be employed—unless driven out of work by the recurrent panics and downturns created by capitalism. Thus the causes of poverty are structural, beyond the responsibility of the poor themselves. The only answer is government action to tame the business cycle or to support jobless families outside the economy. In this century, government has both tried to manage economic conditions to minimize unemployment and established unemployment benefits for people thrown out of work.

The social democratic theory speaks of low wages as well as lack of jobs. Capitalism pays only the wages it needs to attract labor, not those necessary to support families. Again, government and also labor unions must intervene to force employers to pay a "living wage" and perhaps other benefits such as health care. A recent version of this theory says that the answer to poverty is to "make work pay." Poor adults may work little because low wages make jobs scarcely worth the taking. The answer is not only a higher minimum wage but subsidies for low-paid workers, plus better health care and child care. Then families could make it without resorting to welfare.[17]

Recent liberation theology has applied a similar, quasi-Marxist critique to the world economy. In this view, poor countries outside the West are victimized by economic forces over which they have no control. Globalization enslaves them to international corporations, which extract their wealth and perpetuate their poverty. Against this, the church must ally with the poor and stand for the possibility of change.[18]

—*Social barriers.* Given that currently many of the poor are nonwhite and live in female-headed families, other theories stress social conditions.

The minority poor, it is argued, often are kept out of work by racial dis-crimination. Welfare mothers also may be deterred from working by the fact that their benefits are means-tested: the more they earn, the less they get from the government, making employment a losing game. They also may be barred from working by low skills, lack of child care, or lack of health care for their children if they leave welfare. These impediments figure in church statements on poverty keyed to American conditions. A noted letter on the U.S. economy released by the National Conference of Catholic Bishops in 1986 blamed poverty largely on discrimination against minorities and women.[19]

Much academic research on poverty concentrates on identifying barri-ers like these. Scholars investigate which features of the poor or the con-ditions around them are linked statistically with being poor, jobless, or on welfare. Those outcomes turn out to be likeliest for adults who are non-white, female, low-skill, and supporting many children. Such correlates often are construed to be causal and prohibitive. People subject to such conditions, it is thought, *cannot* work regularly. The Catholic bishops, for example, speak of "children and families who struggle against economic, social, and moral pressures that leave them poor and powerless."[20] On the basis of reasoning like this, most academics have doubted that it is feasi-ble or desirable to enforce work in welfare. This attribution of the prob-lems of the poor to a set of diffuse external impediments is a style of analysis that I call *sociologism.*[21]

—*The evidence.* Experience and research has not been kind to these theories.[22] In the contemporary United States, none of the supposed bar-riers explains nonworking poverty well. The idea, as the Catholic bishops contended, that there is "a chronic and growing job shortage," is implau-sible in an economy that, in recent decades, has generated more new jobs than the whole of Europe.[23] While sufficient jobs still might be unavail-able in a recession, the economy has not suffered a serious downturn in twenty years. Millions of unskilled immigrants, legal and illegal, flock here to take low-paid jobs that, for whatever reasons, most native-born poor adults do not take. Labor economists have abandoned the idea that sheer lack of jobs explains low work levels among the poor.[24] The case for insufficient jobs is stronger in Europe, where a more regulated labor mar-ket inhibits job creation.

A more sophisticated version of that theory maintained that jobs might not be lacking in the aggregate but that most openings demand high skills or are located in the suburbs, while most of the nonworking poor are unskilled or trapped in the inner cities.[25] Research has failed to establish, however, that this "mismatch" has more than a small influence on whether poor adults work. It appears that at least low-paid jobs are commonly available to those seeking them, even to low-skilled workers in the inner cities. Those jobs today often are done by illegal immigrants from Latin America and Asia, many of whom do not even speak English.

The theory that low wages are the problem would be more plausible if work levels among the poor were higher. In New York City a century ago, immigrants and their children slaved long hours for pennies just to stay alive, while the rich lived comparatively leisured lives. For those poor, the solution indeed was to raise wages. That occurred, mainly through economic growth but also through labor union action and government wage regulation. Today, however, the rich usually work many more hours than the poor. It typically was middle-class families, not the poor, that sent more members out to work to stay ahead of inflation in the 1970s and 1980s, a period when real wages stagnated or fell for most people. Today, it is difficult to work steady hours at any legal job and stay poor for long, especially if remaining government benefits are claimed. Some "working poor" still remain, but they are outnumbered by the nonworking poor. In 2001, 8.5 million adults worked at some time in the year, yet remained poor; of these, 2.6 million worked full-time for the full year and about 6 million worked less than that. But 13.7 million did not work at all.[26]

As for discrimination, research paints a complex picture. Employers sometimes do hesitate to hire people from the inner city, but the reason apparently is not racism in the old sense of hostility to nonwhites per se. Rather, employers—some of whom are nonwhite themselves—say they find inner-city employees to be unreliable. At least in the recent tight labor market, employers have been quite willing to hire nonwhite people off welfare, although they still raise concerns about dependability.[27] The disincentive to work that comes from receiving welfare appears important in theory but has little actual influence on whether recipients work. Arranging child care is a trial for mothers, but a literal lack of care rarely keeps them from taking jobs.

This is not to say that barriers are a myth. They may be important in particular localities or for some people. I also do not deny that to guarantee jobs, higher wages, or better health or child care might be desirable in itself. The point is only that lack of such things generally has little influence on whether adults go to work in some job. Providing more of these things, by itself, would have little effect on work levels, although it would reduce poverty. Barriers probably have more influence on the quality of jobs people get *if* they work. Especially, the amount of education workers have strongly affects whether they get a skilled, high-paying job. Thus social inequities cause inequality among workers far more than they cause poverty itself.

I also do not deny that the barriers were once more important than they seem today. Chronic joblessness, Jim Crow laws, and meager public benefits posed far worse hurdles to overcoming poverty before 1960 than they did after, especially in depressed parts of the country. Yet work levels among poor adults ran higher in that era than they do today, in part because lower wages made it far easier to be "working poor." Looking further back, to the Victorian era, the evidence for barriers was still stronger. In that era, most of the population was poor by today's standard, and equal rights for workers, blacks, and women were unknown.

Yet paradoxically, as Joel Schwartz has written, most experts on poverty gave less credence to social causes then than they do today. The Victorians strongly blamed poverty on a lack of personal responsibility—an approach that seems far less defensible then than it might be today. Conversely, most contemporary poverty experts embrace sociologism—the attribution of poverty to many diffuse disadvantages—even though the evidence that barriers prevent working today is weak. Like ships passing in the night, society has become more free, yet expert analysis of society has become more determinist.[28]

—*Culture.* A more hostile theory of the cause of poverty—expressed by some employers who try to employ marginal workers—is that poor adults simply "don't want to work." Supposedly, they lack the work ethic that most Americans cherish. But this too appears to be false. Ethnographers generally find that the poor endorse the same values as the better-off. They also want to work for a living, get through school, support their families, avoid trouble with the law, and so on. These professions appear sincere. But for obscure reasons, the poor often fail to do these things. Of course, most people fail to fulfill all their intentions in life, but for the poor that gap is unusually wide.

To account for this paradox, sociologists in the 1960s developed the idea of a "culture of poverty" that I believe is still valid. This theory held that the seriously poor have orthodox values but feel powerless to live by them. Their belief that opportunity is lacking often discourages them from helping themselves, even though the chance at least to avoid poverty and dependency appears to be widely available. This defeatism reflects not so much the current opportunity structure as the more severe conditions that the poor, or their forebears, faced in earlier generations in this country or in their countries of origin. Especially, it reflects the disorganized families that they often knew as children, in which adults seldom displayed control of their lives. A resigned view of one's chances to succeed thus lives on from one generation to the next, depressing work levels and perpetuating poverty, even in an affluent society where adults generally work at high levels.

The culture of poverty also helps to explain the problems of the poor other than nonwork. Unwed pregnancy and drug addiction would appear to be self-defeating, irrational behaviors for those who adopt them. The idea that people "choose" these lifestyles attributes to them more power to control their lives than, inwardly, the seriously poor appear to have. Rather, the problems result from impulses that people give in to when they feel they have no alternative.[29] That can sound invidious, but there is no attribution of individual blame here. To "find fault" would be to attribute to the poor precisely the capacity to control their lives that appears to be lacking. The culture of poverty is as much a collective force as unemployment or racism, and only collective action can change it.

Until recently, a defeatist culture was abetted by permissive public policies. Programs gave benefits to people on the basis of entitlement—because they were needy and without expecting constructive behavior from them. Government did not enforce the civilities in which poor adults claim to believe, widening the gulf that can separate their intentions from their behavior. That has changed in the past decade.

Catholic statements tend to conflate U.S. poverty with world poverty. Both are blamed on structural injustices linked to the economy that only government can overcome.[30] But the two kinds of poverty are almost opposite in character. The argument that social structure explains poverty in the United States is weak. In developing countries, however, it is strong. In that world, destitution is heavily due to lack of employment, low wages, or other constraints on opportunity. Those constraints in turn reflect misgovernment over centuries, the failure to develop the rule of law and accountable government, and also the failure to develop public education and other opportunities for ordinary people, as the United States did from its founding.

In the United States, sustained poverty is usually dysfunctional; that is, the poor often fail to advance even their own self-interest, let alone society's. But that occurs within a society whose basic institutions are effective and fair, at least by world standards. In the developing world, the situation is reversed. Public institutions are dysfunctional due to government weaknesses, but individual behavior appears largely to be rational. Individuals do whatever is sensible for them in straitened circumstances, although their actions may not be collectively rational. If they can, they come to the United States. They immediately get jobs, and they marvel that anyone is poor for long in this land of plenty.

POVERTY AND POLITICS. Poverty has had a profound effect on American politics.[31] Until 1960 the social democratic vision applied well to the United States, as it did to most of Europe. The lowest class was a working class that was assumed to be employed most of the time. There were unemployed people who could not find work, but for most of them joblessness was an interlude in a generally working life. The chief debate in politics was how to advance the interest of these deserving but underprivileged Americans. The left favored more government efforts, such as those undertaken in the New Deal, to regulate the marketplace in order to promote equality and to support people when they could not work. Government sought to expand opportunity first for workers, then for blacks, other minorities, and women. The right favored a smaller government and a freer economy, arguing that this would generate more jobs and higher incomes for workers. This progressive debate, as I call it, put in question the extent of equality and the meaning of justice, but it took the personal competence of ordinary Americans for granted.

Only in the 1960s did poverty in the current sense become an issue, and then the focus of politics reversed. Competence became more controversial than equality. After the enactment of the civil rights reforms and the Great Society social programs in the 1960s, efforts to promote equality faltered. For almost thirty years, politics tended generally to the right, but not because conservatives won the old, progressive debate about how best to advance working Americans. Big government remained popular. It was rather because controversy shifted to how to assuage the inner city, a new issue that favored conservatives. The core dispute in dependency politics, as I call it, was no longer about equality or justice but about whether one could expect the poor to observe the ordinary civilities that earlier generations took for granted. Earlier, the goal of politics has been the good society; now it was simply good behavior.

Liberals generally said that it was unfair to expect good behavior without first reforming society. Conservatives said that it was fair, and their view prevailed. This reflected public opinion. Voters maintained a commitment to a generous social policy—they still wanted government to save families in trouble. But just as strongly, they rejected the permissive form of liberal policy. They demanded that government enforce the work ethic, the criminal law, and standards in the schools. Conservatives proved more willing to do that than liberals, despite their traditional fear of public power. Starting with Richard Nixon, a succession of Republicans rode hard-line views on crime and welfare, among other issues, all the way to the White House. Their reign was interrupted only by Southern Democrats—Jimmy Carter and Bill Clinton—who also were conservative in their attitudes toward crime and welfare, at least for their party.[32]

Commentators on the left say that politics should never have abandoned its focus on equality, that it should have gone on treating the poor as deserving and advancing their interests.[33] If government responded less warmly to the poor than to the working class, they suggested, it was because the former were largely black and Hispanic, the latter white. But the poor from the 1960s on really were different from the earlier proletariat. Social problems have run much higher among them. Questions of "deservingness" were unavoidable. Those concerns could recede only when order was restored in the cities. By the 1990s government started to achieve that. Levels of crime and welfare fell sharply, and the first serious efforts were made to raise achievement levels in urban schools.

Those changes restored some faith in the competence and responsibility of low-income Americans. Then attention reverted toward the progressive question of how to advance equality among workers. That issue favors liberals, and the agenda shifted back to the left. Doing more to help "working families" is now popular. While a Republican is again in the White House, he had to advocate "compassionate conservatism" to get there. President George W. Bush's subsequent proposals in social policy have been moderate. The welfare state is back on the march.

IN SUMMARY. The controversial poverty in America is among working-age adults and their children who remain poor for more than two years at a stretch. Although often such poverty is initially due to unwed childbearing, more often it is due to the lack of regular employment among poor parents, both mothers and fathers. Nonwork, in turn, appears for the most part to be due not to barriers outside the poor but to a defeatist psychology in which work and other proprieties are affirmed in principle but not in practice. Poverty in the developing world is much more structural and less dysfunctional. Finally, the politics of poverty places serious constraints on the pursuit of equality. A liberal agenda assumes a working population. Work levels among the poor must rise to something like the levels typical of the general population or serious proposals to redistribute income or other advantages cannot be made.

WHAT SHOULD WE DO?

The theological basis of this analysis is what the gospels suggest that we should do about poverty. The institutional church asserts that economic poverty is a priority in the Bible, that helping the poor deserves preference over other social concerns, and that the poor are to be aided in a non-judgmental way, with no questions asked about their behavior. In the words of the Catholic bishops, "A constant biblical refrain is that the poor must be cared for and protected and that when they are exploited, God hears their cries"; therefore, they say, "A community is measured by its treatment of the powerless." The standard is the one Jesus sets for the last judgment: it is only those who have helped the destitute who will go to heaven. Ron Sider puts it more bluntly: if the affluent "do not feed the hungry and clothe the naked, they go to hell."[34] It is a chilling prospect that few in government have dared to question.

I think that all of these positions are greatly exaggerated. A close reading of the New Testament gives little warrant for them. There is no preference for the poor, only a lively concern for them as well as other people in trouble. Jesus does help the needy and commands his followers to do so, but he has other concerns, which are not economic, and he is not undemanding toward those he helps. Three priorities for dealing with poverty, I think, emerge from Jesus' interactions with people in the gospels: sustenance, community, and autonomy.

SUSTENANCE. First, Jesus tries to aid people in immediate, practical ways. He spends much of his ministry helping people in trouble, yet he does not concentrate on poverty as such. Virtually everyone in biblical times may have been poor by our standards, but people with unusually low incomes for his society are not an obvious priority of his. Indeed, he says very little about the poor in this sense. He never suggests that low income per se is an emergency or that the rich owe the poor some general recompense, such as a redistribution of income, wealth, or opportunity. Those are modern ideas.[35] The Israel of his day was too primitive for poverty as such to be unusual or controversial.

Jesus' largest act of redistribution was, on two occasions, to feed thousands of people who had followed him out into the wilderness without food.[36] For Jesus, this was an act of compassion, not of justice: "They were harassed and helpless, like sheep without a shepherd."[37] Many of these people were probably not poor by the standards of their own society.

Jesus actually expresses skepticism about the alms giving that was endorsed by official Judaism in his day. Meeting the material needs of others is one way to get to heaven, he suggests, but so is welcoming the stranger or visiting people who are ill or in prison. In other places, Jesus says that the blessed will be those who have behaved well in unspecified ways or who have confessed him as their savior.[38] Jesus sometimes tells his followers to give to the poor, but he wants them to do it in secret, not for public show. The focus is on their spiritual welfare more than on the needs of the poor. Jesus remarks ironically that "you always have the poor with you, and whenever you will you can do good to them." He *opposes* "doing good" in this worldly sense.[39]

If there is a "preferential option" in the gospels, it is for the distressed rather than the poor. People come to Jesus because they are troubled in various ways. Most of them ask for healing, not for alms. Jesus' world was radically more insecure than ours. Famine, oppression, war, and incurable illnesses were daily realities then, as they are for very few Americans today. These troubles did not follow automatically from low income; poverty merely made suffering them more likely. In Jesus' world, the poor were considered to be those who, through some misfortune, could not maintain their accustomed places in society, not those who were low-income in today's sense.[40]

Jesus is more solicitous of the "poor in spirit" than the economically poor. He is not against wealth, but far from believing in material goods, he advises his followers to prefer "treasures in heaven." They should give away their property, even abandon their families, and follow him. Seek the bread of life, not the bread of this world. Seek not comfort in this life but love of God and neighbor, the better to be blessed in the next life. He who saves his life will lose it, while he who gives it up will gain it.[41] Such appeals would motivate monks and nuns to embrace lives of renunciation in the centuries to come.

When he does help people, Jesus expects them to play a role in overcoming their problems. He does not counsel self-help. On the other hand, he does not save nameless poor people who other people tell him are in trouble, as today's advocates of the poor expect government to do, nor does he tell his followers to do so. He does not assume that the poor cannot handle their lives. He is *responsive* to them rather than *protective*. The distressed generally have to approach him personally and *ask* for help.[42] "Ask and you will receive," he tells them. Sometimes, indeed, it takes persistent cries for help to get Jesus' attention, and he suggests that God responds similarly.[43] He also asks petitioners directly what they want, and he expects an answer. He is offended if they make no response, or if they try to get his help without facing him.[44]

Jesus also tells many of those he heals that their own "faith" has saved them. Although he helps them, they also have to accept him. He is not a magician who saves people in spite of themselves. They have to "believe," which for Jesus means not just to trust him but to affirm the meaningfulness of life in a wider sense; those who do this save themselves.[45] Faith, of course, is a gift of God, yet Jesus assumes that we can be open to it. In short, he demands authenticity and integrity from those he aids. At a deep level, they must know what they want, and they must believe that life or God can give it to them. When they make those affirmations, Jesus then affirms them.

Jesus seems to be indifferent to economic poverty and inequality as such. He has more concern for the competence of the poor, and in this he resembles the contemporary economist Amartya Sen. To be poor does not mean just to suffer material destitution, Sen says, but to lack the capacity to affect one's life in many respects. To relieve destitution, therefore, society must do more than raise incomes; it must foster the capabilities of the poor.[46] Two millennia earlier, Jesus seems to think similarly. While relieving distress, he seeks also to promote autonomy and responsibility. He does not want his followers to be passive recipients of his bounty but active participants in their own salvation.

COMMUNITY. Today's approach to poverty focuses too narrowly on economic deprivation. In the biblical tradition, concern is at least as great for the separation of the poor from mainstream society. The poor are not simply needy, they are *outcasts*. This is because they are seen to have violated social mores, reflecting the same concerns about "deservingness" that still surround poverty today.

The institutional church and most commentators that I have read interpret Jesus' position as taking the side of the poor against mainstream society. The onus for bringing the poor back into the community rests entirely on the nonpoor, who must change or abandon the moral standards that now exclude the outcasts. They must ask no questions about whether the poor are "deserving," but simply provide for their needs. The Catholic bishops, for instance, reject the ideas that people are poor primarily because they do not work or have children that they cannot support, calling such notions "misunderstandings and stereotypes."[47]

But the idea that Jesus identifies with the poor in preference to other people cannot be supported from the gospel accounts. He himself was neither poor nor privileged, but born into the middle ranks of his own society.[48] Certainly, he befriends the marginalized as few in his society dared to do. That drew the eye in his time, as it does in ours. But he also has a ministry to the rich. He recruits Levi the tax collector as a disciple, he befriends a scribe and a rich young man, and he spends much of his time interacting with Pharisees, Sadducees, and other members of the elite. He heals all manner of people, with apparent indifference to whether they are rich or poor. They include Peter's mother-in-law, the servant of a Roman centurion, and the children of leading citizens.[49]

The indulgent side of his gospel is not preached only to the poor, nor the demanding side only to the rich. Both classes hear the whole gospel. Jesus' manner varies with his audience, but not his message. To the people he speaks in parables, while with the religious lawyers he debates the law. Nobody gets off easily. To the masses he promises the kingdom of heaven, but he also tells them that they are the "light of the world" and that they "must be perfect, as your heavenly Father is perfect."[50] The parable of the talents suggests that even those with the least resources are expected to use them for good purposes. If they do not, "to every one who has will more be given, but from him who has not, even what he has will be taken away"—the *reverse* of redistribution.[51] Jesus calls his disciplines to love one another, not to love the poor by preference. The "sheep" that Peter is told to feed include all of humanity.[52]

Jesus attacks the religious elites fiercely for their arrogance, legalism, and elitism. They are "blind guides" who have "neglected the weightier matters of the law, justice and mercy and faith." The first shall be last and the last first.[53] But the common interpretation that Jesus took the side of the poor against the elites is mistaken. In upbraiding the leaders, Jesus is concerned as much for *their* welfare as he is for the downtrodden. He wants *them* to be saved, and for this he has to pierce their complacency. The very fact that he criticizes them is an implied compliment. He does not give up on them. He presumes that they take their own moral tradition seriously. In the gospel accounts, they clearly do. Pharisees and Sadducees duel with Jesus seeking to justify themselves. Not all resist him. Hearing his attacks on the Pharisees and Sadducees, a lawyer remarks ruefully, "Teacher, in saying this you reproach us also."[54] Jesus has their attention.

If Jesus had opposed the elites, he would have treated some other group as the true representatives of the society, as Marx treated the working class. But he leaves the existing leaders in charge. Except for asides remarking that leaders pile "heavy burdens" on others and "devour widows' houses," Jesus says nothing concrete about what they have done that is so bad.[55] Nor does he tell them in any detail what they should do instead. He calls for no program to abolish poverty or inequality. Rather, he wants leaders to show a livelier concern for the less fortunate. They should see themselves as servants of their societies, rather than as served by them.[56] But he leaves policy to them, subject only to their accountability to God.[57]

In this he resembles John the Baptist and the prophets. In the Old Testament, to be sure, prophets' attacks on injustice, sexual immorality, and shallow piety are more pointed and specific than in the New Testament. From all we know, poverty in ancient Israel was largely impersonal in origin, due to political and economic constraints, like that of the third world today. Nevertheless, the prophets and Jesus focus on the moral shortcomings of leaders as individuals, not on the "structural" inequities spoken of by modern social critics. Nor is redistribution called for. Throughout the Bible, the charge is that leaders have permitted injustices to occur because they have lost their relationship to God. Reestablish that tie, Jesus and the prophets say, and justice will follow in unspecified ways.[58]

Nearly all the petitioners that we read of approaching Jesus appear more "deserving" than many poor people are likely to seem to us today. They are victims of circumstances. Typically, they suffer from dread diseases that were not of their own doing. Their poverty seems to be narrowly economic in character, again like that of the third world; the dysfunctional patterns seen in American poverty are not conspicuous. But despite this, Jesus does not treat suppliants as innocent victims. As I noted above, he expects them to *ask* for his help and to show *faith*. And after he has healed them, he usually *admonishes* them. Typically, he wants them to discharge the religious rituals connected with healing, or he tells them not to publicize what he has done for them.[59]

In two cases he tells them not to sin again, and in another instance he remarks that healing and forgiveness are the same.[60] That suggests that some of those he saved were not innocent. This does not mean that he blames them for their problems or refuses to help; he does help them. The admonitions come after he has healed them, not before. It is precisely those who are forgiven, who receive grace, who are empowered to admit their own shortcomings without fear. Nevertheless, he expects his followers to "do the right thing."

The best indication we have in the gospels of how Jesus would respond to today's seriously poor occurs at the Pool of Bethesda in Jerusalem. The legend was that an angel periodically troubled the waters of the pool, and then whoever got into it first was healed of any infirmities. Jesus encounters a man who has been lying by the pool ill for thirty-eight years waiting to get in. He must have lived by begging. Jesus first confronts him with a demand to *ask*: "Do you want to be healed?" The man does not answer. Rather, he complains that no one will help him into the pool when the angel comes. But to complain is not the same as to ask. The man cannot imagine why what *he* wants should matter. It is the defeatism, the denial of agency, that is typical of the underclass. Jesus ignores his complaint; instead he abruptly commands, "Rise, take up your pallet, and walk." Startled, the man gets up. He is *healed*. Later, Jesus confronts him again, with the *admonition* "See, you are well! Sin no more, that nothing worse befall you."[61] It is not the unjudging solicitude recommended by the institutional church. But nevertheless, Jesus did do for this man what he needed. When people refuse to take responsibility for themselves, the command to function is what they most need to hear.

In Old Testament times, Israel's practices regarding poverty combined generosity with clear demands for functioning. Able-bodied families or individuals who fell on hard times were allowed to borrow money from the community on generous terms, and some food was set aside for widows, orphans, and others who could not provide for themselves. Every effort was made to avoid stigma. But at the same time, the loans were expected to be repaid, and everyone receiving support had to work for it in some way. Elders created jobs if needed to banish idleness.[62]

Given the evenhandedness of Jesus' ministry, he would most likely have endorsed some system like this. He would want government to be forthcoming to those in need, as he was personally. But he would also expect accountability from recipients, and he would maintain ordinary expectations about "deservingness." In Old Testament language, he would not be "partial to the poor" nor "defer to the great."[63]

AUTONOMY. A third belief discernible in the Scriptures is that the poor, like other people, should become autonomous. In the biblical tradition, autonomy does not mean freedom in the sense that prevails in modern society—the license to do whatever one wants. Rather, to be free is to obey God's will and nothing else. It is to resist unjust authority but also to avoid sin, which meant enslavement to impulse. In the Episcopal phrase, God's "service is perfect freedom."[64] It is one of several senses in which those who would be free must first be bound.

Jesus gives the classic statement of this ideal during his temptation. When he is hungry and the devil offers him food, he responds, "Man shall not live by bread alone, but by every word that proceeds from the mouth of God." Again, when Satan offers him power in return for his allegiance, he responds, "You shall worship the Lord your God, and him only shall you serve." Jesus displays his autonomy by being utterly faithful to God and his own sense of mission and completely unbound by the material concerns and petty proprieties of his own society. The Christian ideal, Paul wrote, was to become "mature" in this same way, to achieve "the stature of the fullness of Christ."[65]

This kind of ideal is suspect to the institutional church because it justifies the sort of rules about good behavior that often marginalize the poor. In our day, as in biblical times, many of the poor have visibly failed to observe God's commandments. Jesus, accordingly, often is thought to have attacked or repealed the "law," in the sense of social mores, precisely in order to incorporate society's outsiders.

He does strongly advocate mercy and forgiveness. He counsels his followers to judge not that they be not judged. Those whom God forgives should likewise forgive others. He practices forgiveness himself, for example, by absolving a woman he encounters of sexual sins. In the great parable of the prodigal son, he suggests that a loving God responds more warmly to those who repent, like the prodigal, than to those, like the prodigal's dutiful older brother, who never stray from the straight and narrow.[66]

But despite this, Jesus does not question the moral law itself. He says he comes to fulfill it, not to abolish it. His followers are to be those who do the will of their Father in Heaven, not those who do not.[67] Jesus was, after all, an observant Jew, although he interpreted his tradition liberally. The laws that he questions are cultic rules governing what Jews could eat and forbidding healing on the Sabbath. That brings him into sharp conflict with the religious authorities, as does his driving the money changers out of the temple.[68] But he never questions the more important laws governing social behavior, which have much more to do with stigmatizing the poor. He calls on his followers to observe love of God and love of neighbor, and he specifically embraces the golden rule and the Ten Commandments, with their strictures against theft, murder, and adultery.[69]

Jesus seems to imagine a world in which both mercy and the law are important. People are to be forgiven their shortcomings, even seventy times seven, but they must seriously repent each time.[70] And however often they are forgiven, the law remains in being. As Paul later wrote, the law itself has only the power to condemn. People become aware of sin precisely through confrontation with the law, because they cannot satisfy it. Salvation comes by another route—by unmerited grace, independent of any "works" or desert. Yet the law is not evil. It remains a valid statement of God's will. One cannot *just* be saved. One must first seriously *try* to be "deserving."[71] One can reach the New Testament only by traveling through the Old. To forgive people without first expecting good behavior is to offer them what Dietrich Bonhoeffer called "cheap grace."[72] Thus, in another sense, those who would be free must first be bound.

Scriptures also specifically affirm the obligation to work that is at the core of the poverty debate. From the fall in the Garden of Eden, God commanded humans to work. Jesus says that he works alongside the Father.[73] Paul cites his own labors as an example to others. Some of his followers imagined that they need not work, because Jesus' second coming was imminent. Paul retorts that they must earn their own living, for "if any one will not work, let him not eat."[74] That command, Michael Harrington wrote, is "the basis of the political economy of the West."[75]

IN SUMMARY. The gospels suggest that we should have concern for the poor, but with attention to actual distress rather than low income or inequality per se. And along with relieving need, we should enhance the agency of the poor. We should hold them, like other people, responsible for themselves. We are to forgive people their trespasses while nevertheless maintaining reasonable expectations about good behavior. The Good News of the gospels is for the poor, but so are the demands. Jesus' ideal is a society in which both rich and poor seek faithfully to fulfill God's will. He is much less concerned about the precise economic arrangements.

The Role of Government

The political basis of this analysis is the special role of government. In responding to poverty, policymakers should be guided by the general precepts suggested above, but they also must respect the distinctive imperatives of public action.

The Bible says little about politics or government. It was written in a predemocratic age, and Israel's chief gifts were not in this area. In New Testament times, Israel was a colony of Rome. Thus to Jesus as to the prophets, government seemed distant and unaccountable. All of them criticized its moral shortcomings; none thought that it could be much better than it was.

Even in the Bible, however, some positive images of government occur. In the Old Testament, David is the image of the able ruler, who, nonetheless, is accountable for his sins.[76] In the gospels, the Roman authorities appear in a favorable light. The centurion who asks Jesus to cure his slave is an image of civility. Pontius Pilate, although he condemns Jesus to death, expresses a laudable concern for keeping order in a fractious Jerusalem. The Romans are bemused spectators of the religious enthusiasms of the Jews, but they are necessary for all that. Jesus is far more tolerant of them than of the Jewish religious authorities. He tells his followers to "render to Caesar the things that are Caesar's." Still more firmly, Paul endorses the authorities as "instituted by God." Christians should obey them and pay taxes, not only out of prudence but "for the sake of conscience."[77]

And the great age of political development was beginning. Rome achieved a government of laws and—at least before the imperial period—greater political accountability than any previous large polity. Following Rome's example, the nations of western Europe would eventually evolve monarchies and then democracies of an enlightened character. Americans take these developments as their birthright. It has become conceivable today, as it seldom is in the Bible, for society to use government to pursue God's will.

Moreover, most civic traditions in the United States were religiously inspired. Of the several political traditions that formed the country, the most ambitious was that of the New England Puritans. Although they came to these shores chiefly for religious liberty, they governed themselves in a strenuous manner that placed collective goals ahead of personal freedom. Their descendants spread that moralistic style across much of the northern part of the country. Those states would become the best-governed in the nation.[78] They would take the lead in developing the complex reciprocity policies that now dominate national welfare policy.[79]

But government's moral pretensions still must be limited. Leaders cannot directly live out the ideals of the Sermon on the Mount. They are responsible for other people, and they are constrained by political prudence. They can do only things for which there is political support, and they must compromise with opponents. Even when they can act on social problems, they must do so at one remove, paying officials to serve the poor or motivating private bodies to do so. Thus government can combat poverty on a large scale, but it cannot do so as directly and effectively as individuals can by helping people they know personally. Public action also involves moral dangers. Government can act only by forcing the public to pay taxes. It must punish lawbreakers. Some welfare policy ideas involve governing the lives of the recipients, as I discuss below. At some level, policymakers always have blood on their hands. [80]

Because of such dilemmas, an ethic for policymaking must stress accountability rather than intention. Policymakers cannot just do what they think is right, blaming a bad outcome on others or leaving the results to God. Rather, they must do what works out best in practice. They must operate by what Max Weber called an "ethic of responsibility" rather than an "ethic of ultimate ends."[81] In social policy, they must do not what feels good, but what actually improves outcomes for those they are trying to help.

Some think that the church should avoid these compromises. Perhaps it should eschew worldly power, especially the evil business of coercing citizens and making war on other nations. Perhaps the church should live out the vision of unjudging solicitude recommended by the institutional church, while leaving the enforcement of good behavior entirely to government.[82] To accept this sort of separation between ethics and politics seems to me small-minded and unwarranted by Scripture. The Christian ethic, if it is serious, must apply in some form to all of human experience, including statesmanship. Coercion should be viewed as regrettable in God's eyes, but if it is necessary to rule, it is nevertheless affirmed.[83]

Some would say that the "fallen" quality of government action in moral terms can explain all of the divergence between biblical prescriptions and what we actually do for the poor. If we are more severe toward them than seems ideal, perhaps this is only because government must defer to a suspicious public opinion or serve private interests.[84] I think this lets the theologians off the hook too easily. If our policy seems questionable, that is probably due in the first instance to how we understand the religious prescriptions. Politics is secondary. Theology is still the queen of the sciences, and we must get it right.

Policies

I now use these premises about poverty, biblical ethics, and public ethics to assess the three principal approaches to antipoverty policy that have appeared in American politics in recent decades: entitlement, self-reliance, and reciprocity.

ENTITLEMENT

"Entitlement" means the policy of giving aid to the needy on the basis of economic criteria that say nothing about "deservingness."[85] While the leading instance was the traditional form of AFDC, the controversial family aid program, much the same approach has characterized other means-tested social programs, including food stamps and Medicaid and also education and training programs for the disadvantaged. In all of these programs, a benefit or service has been offered to those eligible, but no official notice is taken of whether recipients attempt to overcome their problems. None of the programs contained serious work requirements.

These programs are distinct from the much larger social insurance programs that cover the bulk of the population. In Social Security, Medicare, and unemployment insurance, benefits are based on previous contributions rather than means-tested. Social insurance has an implicit work test, since the contributions come from payroll taxes, paid by the beneficiaries or their employers.

The institutional church has consistently favored higher spending and benefits in all these programs. In the 1960s and 1970s, the churches supported the expansion of AFDC to cover more of the working poor. Welfare would have become a guaranteed income for much of low-income America had the proposals passed Congress. In these debates, church voices were the most liberal and the most insistent.[86] Religious liberals affirmed the social democratic vision of poverty, which blamed it entirely on unjust social structures, and the idea that the poor have a priority in the gospels. Such feelings have helped to promote a vast growth in social spending since the mid 1960s. Later, the religious right became a force in politics, but it has never had the same presence in national welfare debates.

The increase in spending unquestionably served the sustenance goal of antipoverty policy. Higher income transfers sharply cut the poverty rate among the elderly and disabled. Whether welfare spending reduced family poverty is less clear, but AFDC did provide a minimum income on which many single mothers relied, although the benefits usually were well below the poverty level. Federal education and training programs also recorded some good effects on their clients, according to evaluations, although they were small. From a biblical viewpoint, these gains from government largesse—in themselves—can only be good.

Entitlement did not, however, generally advance the goals of community or autonomy. Although social insurance beneficiaries can claim respectability because they earn their benefits, traditional welfare does not confer a similar status on its clients.[87] Rather, the proliferation of means-tested programs and benefits tended to isolate low-income areas from mainstream society by allowing them to live apart from it.

The expansion of means-tested programs without work requirements was part of a larger reorientation of federal social policy from class to disadvantage. Up until 1960, federal programs aimed chiefly to ameliorate class differences in the social democratic sense—the gulf in earnings and wealth between the rich and the working class that arose from capitalism. That sort of division could be assuaged by the private efforts of people to get ahead or by public efforts to equalize rewards or improve opportunities for the less privileged. Which approach to favor had been the great issue in progressive politics. Either approach assumed that ordinary people could be held responsible for themselves and their families.

After 1960 serious poverty became a central issue in American politics. This was partly because poor families—especially blacks from the South—had migrated from rural areas to cities, where they were more visible. Now federal policymakers focused less on class than on the "disadvantaged," a term with connotations similar to poverty. In addition to low income, the disadvantaged experienced problems of functioning that impaired their ability to seize the traditional opportunities to get ahead—limitations of education and English literacy as well as the problems of work readiness and family life found among the long-term poor. Programs to serve the disadvantaged included not only entitlement income programs, such as AFDC and food stamps, but the compensatory education and training programs already mentioned.

The reasoning and rhetoric surrounding these programs was sociological in the same sense as most academic research. The problems that the programs addressed were not attributed to their clients but rather to the adverse conditions surrounding them. That approach was easy to justify because the disadvantaged largely meant members of racial minorities, and occasionally women, who in the 1960s were widely seen as oppressed by discrimination. The effect was to shift responsibility for social problems entirely to society. The disadvantaged waited passively for their problems to be solved by others. Politically, one could express sympathy toward them, but not criticism. They could be helped, but not obligated.

A new class system emerged, defined as much by functioning as finances. The rich were now those who, whatever their income, could assume responsibility for themselves and others. The poor were those who were not responsible, for reasons that referred back to an inequitable social structure. But this was to treat as involuntary differences in coping ability what previously had carried moral value. Upstanding qualities had been reckoned as virtues; they now were treated as privileges, a reflex of background.[88] Conversely, those who behaved irresponsibly were not criticized but understood to be responding to their various disadvantages. Much as in academic research, a diffuse determinism eclipsed traditional notions of moral responsibility.

This is not to say that actual welfare administration was lax. In reaction to growing welfare rolls, Washington and the states toughened welfare eligibility requirements, placing rising paperwork burdens on recipients.[89] Nor did most members of disadvantaged groups claim the permission given to them to act out. Most minorities and women continued to get ahead largely by their own efforts, as ordinary people had always done. Due to that effort and equal opportunity policies, the 1960s and 1970s witnessed the emergence of a sizable black middle class, while women ascended to heights of professional success never seen before. But in politics and in media and academic commentary, one could no longer *expect* these groups to function. Only those who were not disadvantaged had a clear obligation to behave well. That largely meant white men.

The institutional church favored these changes, which embodied a preference for the poor. Although in the world, the traditional, largely white male elite continued to hold sway, in the seminaries that hierarchy was inverted. Feminist theologians read the Bible in antipatriarchal ways, while white male candidates for the ministry found themselves viewed by faculty and other students with suspicion. In activist churches, well-to-do members were welcomed mainly for their contributions to anti-poverty missions, not for themselves. Fundamentalist churches rejected these tendencies, but they had less influence on cultural elites and on policymaking.[90]

The shift in social policy thus led to a general redistribution of responsibility in the culture, at least at a rhetorical level. This may have been more important than economic redistribution. In an affluent society, few suffer hardship but many complain about how they are treated. The chief goods to be allocated are no longer economic but psychic, especially the right to blame one's problems on others. The idea of disadvantage that rationalized federal social policies gave the protected groups and their leaders a license to complain, and they seized it. Charges of racism and other denials of equal opportunity resounded through the culture. In part, the lesser responsibility demanded of members of the out groups reflected the notion that they were less competent. They had to be shielded from the full demands of the society, leaders tacitly assumed, lest they fail to meet them. Only white men could not claim victimhood. They were the residual group against whom all claims were made. They were condemned to strength.[91]

The prophet Isaiah spoke of all nations flowing to the house of the Lord, while Jesus said that when he was lifted up he would draw all peoples to himself.[92] In a political way, that happened. Inspired by a diffuse religious earnestness, Washington became a fount of benefits for downtrodden groups, not only in this country but around the world. Private foundations and other nonprofit bodies—still headed for the most part by white men—play a similar role. What the establishment gives is not so much money as a matchless ability to take responsibility for groups and nations that feel helpless, while overlooking their shortcomings. To "do the right thing" was precisely to help without judgment. As Bonhoeffer remarks, "The world was Christianized, and grace became its common property."[93]

But however well-intentioned, the vast aid system was a triumph for the world rather than the Kingdom. The masterful justified themselves by taking care of the less competent, while the latter often took what was offered with little intention of improving their lives. The fact that churches promoted generosity to the poor gave it a fresh mandate. To liberal theologians, the rich stood under judgment; they could escape damnation only by transferring much of their wealth to the needy. In God's eyes, not they but the poor were entitled. During hearings on welfare reform, one welfare rights representative told a Senate committee that government was "supposed to take care of" poor people, and if it did not, "God isn't going to stand for it."[94]

To the institutional church, the "community" included only the poor, whom God has preferred over others, and groups that serve them on a nonjudgmental basis. Only they, strictly speaking, could be part of the Christian fellowship.[95] The rich were to be the servants of the poor but to have no claims of their own. That was official alms giving of just the kind Jesus criticized. But so one-sided a vision of community was bound to fail. A community more worthy of the name must include both rich and poor. This would require that both classes be able to count on *each other* for some things. In some respects, the rich would have to become less responsible for the poor, while the poor became more responsible for themselves and others. The poor would have to bear some obligations that they were truly accountable for and could not shift to the society.[96]

As for the autonomy goal, here too entitlement was lacking. Far from enforcing timeless standards of right and wrong, federal programs exempted needy people from any need to meet many of those standards. Was this merciful—or permissive? Dietrich Bonhoeffer wrote:

> The justification of the good has been replaced by the justification of the wicked; the idealization of good citizenship has given way to the idealization of its opposite . . . ; the forgiving love of Jesus . . . has been misrepresented, for psychological or political reasons, in order to make of it a Christian sanctioning of anti-social "marginal existences." . . . And good, in its citizen-like sense, was held up to ridicule.[97]

It matters that Bonhoeffer was a German—from a political culture oriented to dutifulness. In rights-oriented America, the churches did indeed neglect citizenship. They championed the most ambitious extensions of social rights, without corresponding obligations.

Entitlement was politically unsustainable. A backlash came. From the early 1970s, states allowed AFDC benefits, which they controlled, to decline in value in real terms, because the program was so unpopular. The election of Ronald Reagan as president in 1980 and, even more, the advent of a Republican Congress in 1994 signaled the repudiation of entitlement, at least in cash aid. The objection was much less to the principle of aid or the cost of programs than to their one-sided character. The eventual result was the demand for reciprocity that now animates national welfare policy.

SELF-RELIANCE

As an antipoverty strategy, the opposite of entitlement is self-reliance. By this I mean the proposals of conservatives to cut back or deny aid to the needy. This position rests partly on the principled belief that redistribution of wealth is wrong, a violation of property rights.[98] But more important is the practical contention that denying or reducing aid would actually reduce poverty.

The older version of this argument, made in the progressive era, focused on the macroeconomy. A smaller government, it was claimed, would permit lower taxes and less regulation and so generate more jobs and higher wages for average Americans. Conservative critics of the Catholic bishops' letter on the economy advised the bishops to place more trust in the free-market system, which had generated unparalleled wealth with only a limited public role, although they also accepted the need for public antipoverty programs. Pope John Paul II himself has criticized the overextension of the welfare state to the point where it displaces the responsibility of other bodies and individuals themselves for social advancement.[99]

The more recent version focuses on the incentives set up by means-tested programs. Welfare and other benefit programs make bad behavior a qualification for support. Those who have children out of wedlock or do not work are rewarded for it, not punished as they once would have been. By changing the social rules, programs make people think that these behaviors make sense, but they turn out to be disastrous. Thus trying to help the poor produces more poverty than if government had done nothing. A more limited version of the case does not oppose all welfare but demands that programs be devolved to localities or private bodies such as churches, which will be more willing than Washington to confront the poor with their shortcomings.[100] Presumably these are conservative local congregations, not the liberal policy bodies that speak for the churches in Washington.

The principled objection to redistribution is the easiest to answer. The God of the Bible does not allow other gods, including property rights. The commandment to love one's neighbor unavoidably involves some sharing of wealth. As to the free-market argument, it is difficult to show that social spending, at least on the American scale, has done much to damage the economy. Countries with welfare states larger than ours, such as Germany, are competitive with us. And public transfers have undoubtedly contributed much to the reduction of poverty.[101]

Evidence for the disincentives argument is also weak. As mentioned, the fact that recipients lose benefits if they work has little apparent effect on whether they go to work. It is also difficult to show that the availability or level of welfare benefits has more than a small influence on whether women have children out of wedlock.[102] Dysfunctional behaviors appear to be driven mainly by a lack of personal control of one's life, not by rational calculation, much as the culture of poverty suggests. Indeed, if the seriously poor were as rational as this theory assumes, they would realize that welfare dependency was a bad deal and avoid it. The most one can say is that welfare helps to finance misbehaviors that occur largely for other reasons.

Thus self-reliance involves clear losses for the goal of sustenance. Does it serve the goal of community or self-reliance any better? Its proponents think so, but that too is doubtful. How can community be served by *not* helping people in need? The problem with entitlement is not that aid is given but that it is unconditional. The devolution theory imagines that at the local level aid programs would somehow be consistent with community, as national programs are not. Federal programs arose historically because local or private aid was insufficient to deal with widespread distress, such as occurred during the Great Depression.

The antigovernment prescription is an attempt to go back to the political economy of the nineteenth century, when government accepted little responsibility for poverty. Given the real achievements of social programs since then, for all their problems, that approach no longer seems defensible from a religious perspective. The institutional church is mistaken to support entitlement but correct to oppose antigovernment conservatism.

A retreat from antipoverty efforts also would be impolitic. Polls and elections make it clear that the public expects the government to take the lead in combating poverty. Serious attempts to curtail that role will be resisted. The election of conservative presidents since Nixon does not mean that the public is disillusioned with big government. Americans voted for Ronald Reagan largely to get stronger leadership and a stronger military, not because they embraced the antigovernment side of Reagan's agenda. The objection, much more, was to entitlement.[103]

RECIPROCITY

The third antipoverty approach is the one that now dominates national and state policy—requiring adult recipients to work in return for aid. This policy goes back to 1967, when Congress attached the first mandatory work programs to AFDC. Recipients judged to be employable were in theory required to participate in the programs as a condition of eligibility for benefits. The requirements were progressively tightened in later years, although they still affected only a minority of welfare mothers.

The Family Support Act of 1988 made more recipients subject to the requirements but allowed most participants to pursue education or training for better jobs rather than working immediately in low-paid positions. When PRWORA transformed AFDC into TANF in 1996, the rules were stiffened further. States were told to have half of their cases engaged in work activities by 2002 or face cuts in their federal welfare funding. Interim participation targets were set to achieve that goal. The activities that counted as work now favored actual employment and excluded most education and training.

The political rationale for work enforcement was suggested above. The public rejects entitlement for the employable, but it also opposes forcing people to work simply by cutting back aid. The voters want families to be aided generously—provided that the parents work alongside the taxpayers.[104] The only way to square this circle is to enforce work in and through welfare itself.

The policy rationale was that mandatory work programs in AFDC were proven to be effective in evaluations of programs from the 1980s and early 1990s. That is, the programs recorded meaningful gains in employment and earnings and reductions in dependency for their clients compared with comparable recipients who were not subject to the requirements. Programs that explicitly demanded work achieved noticeably more than work incentives, which allowed recipients to keep more of their welfare benefits *if* they worked. Voluntary work and training programs showed weaker effects, probably because they could not command the same effort from their clients. By the late 1980s, most experts believed that welfare work programs were worth expanding. That expansion occurred initially in the Family Support Act (FSA) in 1988 and then, much more sharply, in PRWORA.[105]

Later evaluations made clear that, to maximize their effects, work programs had to enforce participation stringently and expect recipients to take available jobs, even if low paid. Education or training should be allowed only for a short period and only if it focused on actual jobs. Sending recipients to school or to college for long periods generally was not a good investment. Hence TANF's insistence in most cases on actual work instead of education.[106] That insistence amounts to saying that work must be treated first and foremost as an obligation and not as an opportunity or a right.

To date, serious work requirements exist only in TANF. However, weaker requirements exist in food stamps, and localities have instituted work tests in local aid programs that they control. In addition, the success of welfare-work programs has promoted the spread of the idea of reciprocity to other areas of social policy. Some states have required that welfare parents not only work but get their children vaccinated or keep them in school—what is known as "learnfare"—as a condition of aid. Some also are trying to require the absent fathers of welfare families either to make their child support payments or to participate in work programs, on pain of going to prison.

In all of these areas, the most effective programs use case managers to oversee their recipients closely, not only to arrange child care and other needed services but to make sure that clients continue to participate. This style, which I call paternalism, is the antithesis of entitlement. It gets results that programs that offer only benefits and opportunities cannot. Clients react surprisingly warmly to the oversight. The reason goes back to the culture of poverty discussed above. For the most part, what the poor need is not to be taught correct values but to organize their lives to achieve them. Overcoming helplessness requires help but also hassle. Poor adults often need someone "on their case" to be sure they "do the right thing." They need to be admonished in just the way that Jesus admonishes those he helps in the gospels. Paternalism helps close the gap between what the poor want to do and how they actually live.[107]

Although popular with the public and accepted by most recipients, work requirements were stiffly opposed by liberal members of Congress and community groups when they were first proposed in the 1960s and 1970s. These voices asserted that it was punitive to force welfare adults to work when the reasons for nonwork, they believed, lay in the wider society. Those reasons included all the barriers mentioned above, especially inadequate child care. Remove the barriers and improve supports for families, they believed, and work levels would rise without enforcement.[108]

Although swayed by the positive results of experimental programs, most academic experts on poverty also hesitated to enforce work requirements for fear that hardship would result. They preferred to promote employment with new benefits, such as government jobs, rather than to require work as a strict condition of aid. President Clinton's own welfare proposal in 1994 required younger welfare mothers to work after two years on the rolls, with public jobs provided if they could not find their own. PRWORA was more severe and lacked the same guarantees. When congressional Republicans forced the president to sign the act, several academics in senior welfare policy positions resigned from the administration.[109]

Of the liberal forces opposed to work enforcement, the most strident was the institutional church. Representatives of many denominations, Protestant and Catholic, inveighed against work tests in congressional welfare hearings in the 1960s and 1970s. They summoned up images of helpless welfare recipients who would be oppressed, identifying them with the innocent victims who, they believed, are God's special charges. But if the poor had rights against government, the prosperous had no comparable claims; their property was in principle a community resource, to be taxed as necessary to support the needy. By the time of the Family Support Act in the late 1980s, church opposition had cooled somewhat, with some denominations now receptive to mandatory work programs, at least in principle. But even then, they saw them chiefly as new benefits for the recipients and did not embrace the desirability of work enforcement as such.[110]

The most elaborate statement of the church position appears in Catholic tracts that bear on poverty, both papal encyclicals and the American bishops' letter on the economy. The popes and bishops accept that there is an obligation to work, justified on the biblical grounds given above. But they speak of this duty only in the most general terms. On a practical level, they treat work as a right that government must guarantee to willing workers, not as an obligation it can impose. Government must ensure jobs and adequate wages, support families during unemployment, and so on.

That partly reflects the social democratic vision that theologians favor, the view that poverty and nonwork are imposed by the economy. At a deeper level, it reflects the focus of Catholic social teaching on the "dignity" of the human person, an emphasis that is particularly strong in the current pope. To force people to work seems to violate dignity. This causes the church to forbid that women with children be required to work; rather, they should be left free to decide for themselves whether to work.[111] This stance flatly rejects the policy that the government now pursues.

The American bishops' letter on the economy coupled the social democratic vision with greater sociologism than is found in papal statements. The problems of the poor in functioning were faced somewhat more squarely, but, in the sociological style, they were referred back to structural features of the society. The bishops blamed poverty on "institutional relationships [that] distribute power and wealth inequitably" rather than on "differences in talent or desire to work." Like the popes, they posited an obligation to work in general terms, but they also said that the poor must be "empowered" to "participate" by society. So the onus of work was shifted to government. The bishops called for various new benefits that they thought would promote work, including job creation programs, but participation was entirely voluntary. Like the popes, they opposed requiring mothers with young children to work. And they continued to call for higher and more ensured income benefits, with or without work.[112]

Later statements have been more cautious. In an update of the letter issued in 1995, the American bishops struck many of the same themes as before, but they were more agnostic about attributing poverty and inequality to the economy. They also admitted more candidly the role of unwed childbearing and other "immoral behavior" in causing poverty. In a statement to Congress about welfare reform that same year, the U.S. Catholic Conference recognized the need for change and claimed to support values such as "responsibility" and "work." Yet it still resisted "rigid rules and arbitrary time lines" that might put families at risk. Thus it still defended entitlement.[113]

Despite misgivings on the left, the effects of work enforcement have turned out to be remarkably positive. Coupled with excellent economic conditions and increased spending on child care and wage subsidies, work tests have driven the AFDC/TANF rolls down by over 60 percent since their height in 1994. The relative contribution of these factors to the fall is disputed, but the best studies suggest that welfare reform was probably the leading cause.[114]

Most of those who left welfare are working. Work levels among the poor as a whole have soared. In 1993, only 44 percent of poor female family heads with children worked during the year, and only 9 percent worked full-time for the full year. But in 2000, those numbers had jumped to 63 and 20 percent, respectively; in 2001, they fell back to 58 and 17 percent, probably due to the recession.[115] Less sharply, family income is up and poverty rates are down. Meanwhile, other effects on families appear largely positive. If welfare mothers are subject to work requirements, their children tend to do better in school and, in some studies, the mothers are more likely to marry or cohabit with their spouses. The main negative effect has been that teenage children appear more likely to get in trouble after school because working mothers are less available to supervise them.[116]

In reference to my three goals for antipoverty policy, work enforcement took a risk with respect to the goal of sustenance. Some families lost income when they left welfare, especially if they did not work. Despite earnings gains, the loss of AFDC and associated benefits such as food stamps as people left welfare may initially have depressed incomes at the bottom of society.[117] Yet hardship has been uncommon. Clearly more must be done to elevate the incomes of single mothers who have left welfare for work, but the political chances of doing this are vastly improved now that most of the mothers are employed.

The clearest gains have been for the goal of community. John Paul II wrote that work "first and foremost unites people"; it has "the power to build a community."[118] Welfare reform has vindicated that promise. By moving welfare mothers wholesale into the labor force, work enforcement has sharply increased their involvement with mainstream society. Most of these mothers feel better to be working, although managing households and child care is difficult. This achievement, too, is incomplete, as little has been done so far to bring the absent fathers of welfare families in from the cold. Somehow they too must be made to work more regularly in return for more assistance and more contact with their families.

As to the autonomy goal, one can say only that trends are positive. Rates of unwed pregnancy, crime, drug addiction, and other social problems generally have been falling for about a decade. Some of that decrease probably is due to the positive message about individual responsibility given by welfare reform, as well as to more conservative policies in law and child support enforcement.[119] The prosperity of much of the past decade doubtless has contributed as well. Poverty is far from vanquished, but society's greater willingness to enforce, as well as subsidize, good behavior on all these fronts has brought clear progress.

Finally, the reciprocity approach is politically successful. Continued aid combined with work requirements was what the public always wanted out of welfare reform. They are at last getting it. The result of the caseload reduction has not been to cut back the public commitment to the poor, as opponents feared. Rather, as states and Washington have spent less on cash aid to families, they have spent more on child care, other support services, and wage subsidies for low-income workers.[120] Helping working families is *much* more popular than subsidizing the nonworking. So the political climate for antipoverty policy has improved.

Work enforcement is a classic achievement of statecraft—effective rather than feel-good. Many recipients had grown used to an aid system that asked few questions about their private lives. So had welfare administrators, who were rewarded mainly for preventing errors in eligibility and grant payment, not for overseeing the lives of their clients. Few politicians and administrators took delight in disrupting this system. But they saw that they had to do it to break the mold of the inner city and create new chances for progress. That they were able to do it, and with such good effects, is a triumph for government. Indeed, welfare reform seems to me the greatest victory government has won over working-age poverty since it first became an issue forty years ago.

All told, reciprocity emerges as clearly the best approach to aiding the poor through government, at least if one concentrates on working-age individuals. Entitlement and the denial of aid have a place for some elements of the needy in some situations. But given the current preponderance of working-age poor, the gospel injunctions properly understood, and political constraints, giving aid in return for self-help must be our dominant strategy.

TANF and Reauthorization

Finally, what does a biblical perspective suggest about Temporary Assistance for Needy Families, the nation's current welfare law, which Congress will probably reauthorize in 2003 or 2004?

The enactment of TANF in 1996 changed several aspects of welfare policy. I have emphasized the new work requirements, which reflect the reciprocity approach to poverty. Other dimensions of the law, however, reflect the self-reliance approach, which was favored by hard-line conservatives within the new Republican congressional majority.[121] TANF ended the entitlement status of family aid in the budgetary sense, in that all those eligible for benefits were no longer assured of federal funding. Now states received fixed grants from Washington rather than having their spending, however great, matched at specified rates. Federal funding might now run out if demand for aid ran high. TANF also limited families to a total of five years on aid, measured from the signing of the law in August 1996; after that, states would have to fund continued aid themselves. Finally, TANF tried to deter unwed childbearing, a concern of the political right, by allowing states, if they chose, to deny aid to unwed mothers under eighteen and to children born on the welfare rolls. It also offered states a bonus to encourage them to reduce unwed childbearing and otherwise promote marriage as a solution to poverty.[122]

I saw no need for the antigovernment aspects of TANF. I thought that serious work tests, if well implemented, were enough to control dependency. It would be undesirable to deny aid to recipients who were unable to work or to place a time limit on aid for them. If implemented severely, TANF's antigovernment dimensions could be impolitic, since the public clearly expects government to go on helping families unable to fend for themselves.[123] In a biblical light, these provisions contravene the goal of sustenance.

Fortunately, most states have concentrated on enforcing the work requirements. This aspect of TANF was the most popular and also the most feasible. Government already knew how to implement work tests, if it was willing to do so. States have virtually ignored the family provisions. Enforcing marriage was both more controversial and more difficult than work, and programs of clear effectiveness have not yet appeared. States are also spending serious money on new child and health care benefits to promote work. Most have cushioned the impact of work tests and time limits on families, provided recipients are making an effort to work.[124] Effort is precisely what the public, like Jesus, seems to want from people in trouble, not total self-reliance. Thus although TANF stresses both reciprocity and self-reliance, the former has been much the stronger theme at the operating level. Otherwise, the effects of reform, both practical and political, might have been less positive.

Nevertheless, the task of enforcing work in welfare is still far from complete. Nationwide in 2001, only 34 percent of cases met TANF's work participation standards, well short of the 45 percent standard set for that year in the original legislation.[125] The conversion of welfare into a work program still is sharply contested in California and New York, which have the largest caseloads, and in other urban states. In the main, only states with strong good-government traditions, such as Oregon and Wisconsin, have dealt well with all the challenges that reform poses, both for politicians and administrators.[126]

Congress opened hearings on the reauthorization of TANF in 2002. One consensual change will be to eliminate a loophole that weakened the work requirements as first enacted in 1996.[127] The Bush administration also proposed stiffening work tests still further. There would be "universal engagement": all recipients would have to enter activities of some kind within sixty days of entering welfare. The share of recipients that states must have active in work activities would be raised from 50 to 70 percent by 2007. The weekly hours they would have to participate to be considered active would rise from thirty or thirty-five to forty, of which twenty-four would have to be actual work rather than training. The administration also would spend new money on programs to promote marriage.[128]

Democrats wanted to allow more recipients to engage in education and training in place of work, demanded more money for child care, and questioned the need for family programs. While TANF is too successful for its fundamentals to be challenged, there still is substantial opposition among liberal Democrats and community groups to the principle of conditioning aid on work. In the House, seventy Democrats endorsed a plan to gut work tests, and advocacy groups demonstrated against the Bush proposals.[129] These forces also want poverty reduction to become an explicit goal of TANF, as it was not in the original legislation.

In 2002 the Bush proposals passed with little change in the House, where the Republican majority overrode Democratic opposition. In the Senate, Democrats had a one-seat edge and held up action, forcing Congress to defer decisions until 2003. Then in the 2002 elections, the GOP recovered control of the Senate. A more conservative outcome is now likely, but Democrats have sufficient strength, especially in the Senate, to force some compromise with their perspectives.

The institutional church retreated further from its earlier resistance to work tests, limiting its opposition to TANF to details. Unanimously, church groups seconded the idea that poverty reduction should become a goal of TANF. They sought more funding for various support services, especially child care. They strongly urged allowing more education to count toward fulfilling the work tests. But if frontal opposition was lacking, the groups continue to treat the poor as victims of whom little can be expected. The obligation to work is embraced only in the most general terms, if at all. The entire emphasis is on protecting the vulnerable. These poor are not the light of the world, but rather the objects of other people's virtue. The churches continue to side with them against the rest of the community. Although its voice is lower, the official church is still defending the psychic class system of the liberal era, in which the poor were entitled and the rich were obligated to serve them.[130] On the record, this is a recipe for a caste society rather than community.

I think work tests should be embraced rather than resisted. Instead of defending unconditional aid, the friends of the poor should willingly enforce work requirements for the employable up front and then rebuild a generous support system on the other side of entitlement. To that end, I favor the administration's proposals for universal engagement and the twenty-four-hour work standard. The 70 percent participation level and the forty-hour activity standard, however, are too demanding. It will be tough enough to achieve the 50 percent participation rate and the thirty to thirty-five hours a week that TANF originally mandated for 2002. To enforce requirements better, I would also toughen sanctions for noncompliance.[131]

On the other hand, I would still allow some training, provided it was aimed at specific jobs. I would improve support services and wage subsidies for recipients moving into jobs. One goal is to raise incomes, which is one of welfare reform's unfinished tasks. I would also take further steps to both promote and enforce work by absent fathers, the other unfulfilled promise. Fathers must somehow be brought into the emerging new aid system, where people have to work but in return gain a more secure place in the society.[132]

This is a community that could embrace not just the poor and their advocates, but the better-off as well. For the poor will not only be less poor if they work; they will become less alien to other people. That is a vision that is politic, speaks to the real needs of the poor, and advances the gospels' vision of a more unified society.

Notes

1. Mary Jo Bane and I differ in our viewpoints but, just as important, in how far we rely on previous writings on religion and poverty. She speaks out of a long and eminent tradition of Catholic social teaching, although she also criticizes that tradition in some respects. I have learned much from the people mentioned in the acknowledgments and from the limited reading I have been able to do on the subject of our dialogue. But the essentials of my viewpoint are, so far as I have read, entirely my own. I find this quite surprising.

2. I was raised a Presbyterian in a family with New England roots going back to the Puritans. Since 1979 I have attended Episcopal churches in New York City. In the 1970s, in Washington, D.C., I belonged for several years to the Church of the Saviour, a local church strongly focused on missions to the poor. While I differ with Church of the Savior, I owe much to its members. My experience shaped the views I express here. On the origin and philosophy of this church, see Elizabeth O'Connor, *Call to Commitment: The Story of the Church of the Saviour, Washington, D.C.* (Harper & Row, 1963).

3. I do not address secular theorists of ethics who touch on poverty. John Rawls, in *A Theory of Justice* (Harvard University Press, 1971), famously made gains for the least advantaged a criterion for allowing any inequality in society. But it is fair to say that the debate surrounding Rawls and his critics has affected the academic world more than politics or social policy.

4. My earlier books document and advocate this shift. See Lawrence M. Mead, *Beyond Entitlement: The Social Obligations of Citizenship* (Free Press, 1986); Mead,

The New Politics of Poverty: The Nonworking Poor in America (Basic Books, 1992); Mead, ed., *The New Paternalism: Supervisory Approaches to Poverty* (Brookings, 1997).

5. Mead, *New Politics of Poverty*, pp. 57–61.

6. U.S. Bureau of the Census, *Poverty in the United States: 2001*, Current Population Reports, P60-219 (Government Printing Office, September 2002), pp. 5, 21.

7. Robert E. Rector, Kirk A. Johnson, and Sarah E. Youssef, "The Extent of Material Hardship and Poverty in the United States," *Review of Social Economy*, vol. 57, no. 3 (September 1999), pp. 351–87; Christopher Jencks, Susan E. Mayer, and Joseph Swingle, "Who Has Benefited from Economic Growth in the United States since 1969? The Case of Children," in Edward Wolff, ed., *What Has Happened to the Quality of Life in the Advanced Industrialized Nations?* (London: Edward Elgar, 2003).

8. Rebecca M. Blank, *It Takes a Nation: A New Agenda for Fighting Poverty* (Russell Sage Foundation and Princeton University Press, 1997), pp. 22–25; Peter Gottschalk, Sara McLanahan, and Gary Sandefur, "The Dynamics and Intergenerational Transmission of Poverty and Welfare Participation," in Sheldon H. Danziger, Gary D. Sandefur, and Daniel H. Weinberg, eds., *Confronting Poverty: Prescriptions for Change* (Russell Sage Foundation and Harvard University Press, 1994), pp. 93–95; Greg J. Duncan, *Years of Poverty, Years of Plenty: The Changing Fortunes of American Workers and Families* (University of Michigan, Institute for Social Research, 1984), pp. 48–52, 79–81.

9. Blank, *It Takes a Nation*, pp. 22–23.

10. Mary Jo Bane, "Household Composition and Poverty," in Sheldon H. Danziger and Daniel H. Weinberg, eds., *Fighting Poverty: What Works and What Doesn't* (Harvard University Press, 1986), chapter 9.

11. U.S. Census Bureau, March 2002 Annual Demographic Survey, table 13.

12. Ibid., table 2.

13. Ibid., table 17; House Committee on Ways and Means, *2000 Green Book: Background Material and Data on Programs within the Jurisdiction of the Committee on Ways and Means*, 106th Cong., 2d sess., 2000, Committee Print 106–14, 438.

14. To be "unemployed" implies that one is looking for work. In official usage, the unemployment rate is the percent of the labor force (all those who seek work, whether employed or jobless) that is seeking work but has not taken a job. Those who are jobless but are not looking for work are counted as outside the labor force rather than unemployed, even if they say they would like to work. We do not know that the unemployed have found no jobs, only that they have not accepted them. The unemployment rate thus indicates only very roughly the extent to which jobs are lacking for those seeking them. The higher it is, the more likely it is that openings are insufficient for the labor force.

15. Leo XIII, Rerum Novarum: *On the Condition of the Working Classes* (Vatican City, May 15, 1891); John Paul II, Laborem Exercens: *On Human Work* (Vatican City, September 14, 1981); John Paul II, Centesimus Annus: *On the Hundredth Anniversary of* Rerum Novarum (Vatican City, May 1, 1991).

16. For example, Abraham Kuyper, *The Problem of Poverty*, ed. James W. Skillen (Grand Rapids, Mich.: Baker Book House, 1991). This book was first published in 1891, the same year as *Rerum Novarum*.

17. David T. Ellwood, *Poor Support: Poverty in the American Family* (New York: Basic Books, 1988).

18. Gustavo Gutiérrez, *A Theology of Liberation: History, Politics, and Salvation*, trans. and ed. Sister Caridad Inda and John Eagleson (Maryknoll, N.Y.: Orbis Books, 1985).

19. National Conference of Catholic Bishops, *Economic Justice for All: Pastoral Letter on Catholic Social Teaching and the U.S. Economy* (Washington: 1986), sections 170–215.

20. National Conference of Catholic Bishops, *A Decade after Economic Justice for All: Continuing Principles, Changing Context, New Challenges* (Washington: 1995), p. 1.

21. Typical compendiums of poverty research, largely in this style, include Phoebe H. Cottingham and David T. Ellwood, eds., *Welfare Policy for the 1990s* (Harvard University Press, 1989); Christopher Jencks and Paul E. Peterson, eds., *The Urban Underclass* (Brookings, 1991); and Sheldon H. Danziger and Robert Haveman, eds., *Understanding Poverty* (Russell Sage Foundation and Harvard University Press, 2001).

22. The following discussion draws on Mead, *New Politics of Poverty*, chapters 4–7, which give more detailed references.

23. National Conference of Catholic Bishops, *Economic Justice for All*, section 149.

24. Blank, *It Takes a Nation*, chapter 2.

25. William Julius Wilson, *When Work Disappears: The World of the New Urban Poor* (New York: Knopf, 1996); Douglas S. Massey and Nancy A. Denton, *American Apartheid: Segregation and the Making of the Underclass* (Harvard University Press, 1993).

26. U.S. Census Bureau, March 2002 Annual Demographic Survey, table 10.

27. Joleen Kirschenman and Kathryn M. Neckerman, "'We'd Love to Hire Them, But . . .': The Meaning of Race for Employers," in Jencks and Peterson, eds., *Urban Underclass*, pp. 203–32; Harry J. Holzer and Michael A. Stoll, "What Happens When Welfare Recipients Are Hired?" (Georgetown University, May 2000).

28. Joel Schwartz, *Fighting Poverty with Virtue: Moral Reform and America's Urban Poor, 1825–2000* (Indiana University Press, 2000), chapter 5.

29. Statistical research finds that poverty is associated with inefficacy, but the nature of the causal connection is less clear. See Mary Corcoran and others, "Myth and Reality: The Causes and Persistence of Poverty," *Journal of Policy Analysis and Management*, vol. 4, no. 4 (Summer 1985), pp. 516–36; and Mary Jo Bane and David T. Ellwood, *Welfare Realities: From Rhetoric to Reform* (Harvard University Press, 1994), chapter 3.

30. National Conference of Catholic Bishops, *Economic Justice for All*; John Paul II, *Centesimus Annus*.

31. The following draws on Mead, *New Politics of Poverty*, chapters 1–2, 9–11.

32. Thomas Byrne Edsall, *Chain Reaction: The Impact of Race, Rights, and Taxes on American Politics* (Norton, 1991); Peter Brown, *Minority Party: Why Democrats Face Defeat in 1992 and Beyond* (Washington, D.C.: Regnery Gateway, 1991).

33. Robert Kuttner, *The Life of the Party* (New York: Viking, 1987); Theda Skocpol, "Sustainable Social Policy: Fighting Poverty without Poverty Programs," *American Prospect*, vol. 1, no. 2 (Summer 1990), pp. 58–70.

34. National Conference of Catholic Bishops, *Economic Justice for All*, sections 38, 44, 49; Matthew 25:31–46; Ronald J. Sider, *Rich Christians in an Age of Hunger: Moving from Affluence to Generosity* (Nashville, Tenn: W Publishing, 1997), p. xiv. Biblical quotations are taken from the Revised Standard Version.

35. One reason to doubt the centrality of poverty to the Gospels is that references to rich and poor occur overwhelmingly in Luke. There are fewer in Matthew and almost none in Mark or John.

36. Matthew 14:14–21, 15:32–38; Mark 6:34–44, 8:1–9; Luke 9:11–17; John 6:1–14.

37. Matthew 9:36–38.

38. Matthew 10:32–33, 12:36–37, 16:27, 19:29–30, 25:31–46; Luke 9:26, 12:8–9.

39. Matthew 6:2–4, 19:21, 26:8–11; Mark 10:21,14:5–7; John 12:3–8; John R. Schneider, *The Good of Affluence: Seeking God in a Culture of Wealth* (Grand Rapids, Mich.: Eerdmans, 2002), p. 89.

40. B. J. Malina, "Wealth and Poverty in the New Testament and Its World," *Interpretation* vol. 41, no. 4 (October 1987), pp. 354–66.

41. Matthew 5:3, 6:19–21, 10:34–39, 16:24–26; Mark 10:21; Luke 9:23–25, 14:26–33; John 6:26–35, 48–51. See also Johannes Baptist Metz, *Poverty of Spirit*, trans. John Drury (Paramus, N.J.: Paulist Press, 1968).

42. Matthew 8:2–3, 9:27–31,15:22–28, 17:14–18, 20:29–34; Mark 1:40–42, 10:46–52; Luke 5:12–13, 17:12–14, 18:35–43.

43. Matthew 7:7–8; Mark 11:23–24; Luke 11:5–13, 18:2–8.

44. He reacts this way to the man at the Pool of Bethesda, who does not answer his question (John 5:6–8), and to the woman with an issue of blood, who tries to be cured by touching his robe without facing him directly (Mark 5:25–33; Luke 8:43–47); the same impatience does not appear in Matthew 9:20–22.

45. Matthew 9:2, 27–30, 15:28; Mark 5:34, 10:52; Luke 7:50, 9:48, 17:19.

46. Amartya Sen, *Inequality Reexamined* (Russell Sage Foundation and Harvard University Press, 1992).

47. National Conference of Catholic Bishops, *Economic Justice for All*, section 193.

48. Schneider, *Good of Affluence*, pp. 123–27.

49. Matthew 8:5–15, 17:14–18, 19:16–22; Mark 1:30–31, 5:22–24, 35–43, 7:25–30. 9:17–27, 10:17–22, 12:28–34; Luke 4:38–39, 7:2–17, 8:41–42, 49–56, 9:38–43; John 4:46–53, 11:1–44.

50. Matthew 5:13–14, 48.

51. Matthew 25:14–30; Luke 16:10–12, 19:11–26.

52. John 13:34–35, 15:12–17, 21:15–17.

53. Matthew 11:8, 15:3–9, 21:31–32; 23:5–7, 13–28; Mark 7:6–13, 9:35, 10:31, 12:38–40; Luke 7:25, 11:42–43, 13:30, 14:7–11, 18:9–14, 20:46.

54. Luke 11:45.

55. Matthew 23:4; Luke 11:46, 21:47.

56. Matthew 20:20–28, 23:8–12; Mark 10:35–45; Luke 22:24–27.

57. Allen Verhey, *Remembering Jesus: Christian Community, Scripture, and the Moral Life* (Grand Rapids, Mich.: Eerdmans, 2002), p. 368, 396–402.

58. Abraham J. Heschel, *The Prophets: An Introduction* (Harper Torchbooks, 1969).

59. Matthew 8:4, 9:30, 12:16; Mark 1:43–44, 5:19, 43, 7:36, 8:26; Luke 5:14, 8:56; John 5:14, 8:11, 9:7.

60. Matthew 9:2–6; Mark 2:3–11; Luke 5:18–25; John 5:14; 8:11.

61. John 5:2–15.

62. John D. Mason, "Biblical Teaching and Assisting the Poor," *Transformation*, vol. 4, no. 2 (April 1987): 1–14.

63. Leviticus 19:15.

64. *The Book of Common Prayer* (New York: Seabury Press, 1979), p. 57.

65. Matthew 4:3–4, 8–10; Ephesians 4:13.

66. Matthew 6:14–15, 7:1–5, 18:23–35; Luke 6:37, 41–42, 7:36–49, 15:11–32, 16:1–9; John 8:3–11.

67. Matthew 5:17–20, 12:48–50; Mark 3:31–35; Luke 8:19–21, 11:27–28, 16:16–17.

68. Matthew 9:14–17, 12:1–14; Mark 2:18–28, 3:1–6, 7:1–23; Luke 5:33–39, 6:1–11, 7:33–34, 11:37–41, 13:10–16, 14:2–6; John 5:9–12, 16–18, 7:23, 9:14–16.

69. Matthew 7:12, 22:36–40; Mark 10:19, 12:29–31; Luke 10:25–28.

70. Matthew 18:21–22; Luke 17:3–4.

71. Romans 7–8; Galatians 3–4.

72. Dietrich Bonhoeffer, *The Cost of Discipleship* (New York: Macmillan, 1963), chapter 1.

73. Genesis 3:17–19; John 5:17.

74. Acts 20:34; 1 Corinthians 4:12; Ephesians 4:28; 1 Thessalonians 4:11; 2 Thessalonians 3:7–12.

75. Michael Harrington, *The New American Poverty* (Holt, Rinehart, and Winston, 1984), p. 98.

76. 2 Samuel 23:3–4.

77. Matthew 8:5–13, 22:16–22; Mark 12:4–17; Luke 7:2–10, 20:21–25; Romans 13:1–7.

78. David Hackett Fischer, *Albion's Seed: Four British Folkways in America* (Oxford University Press, 1989); Daniel J. Elazar, *American Federalism: A View from the States*, 3d ed. (New York: Harper & Row, 1984), chapter 5.

79. Lawrence M. Mead, "Welfare Reform: The Institutional Dimension," *Focus*, vol. 22, no. 1 (special issue 2002), pp. 39–46; and *Government Matters: Welfare Reform in Wisconsin* (Princeton University Press, 2004), chapters 11–13.

80. Reinhold Niebuhr, *Moral Man and Immoral Society* (Scribners, 1960); Verhey, *Remembering Jesus*, pp. 317–21.

81. "Politics as a Vocation," in Max Weber, *From Max Weber: Essays in Sociology*, ed. and trans. H. H. Garth and C. Wright Mills (Oxford University Press, 1958), pp. 115–28.

82. John Howard Yoder, *The Politics of Jesus:* Vicit Agnus Noster (Grand Rapids, Mich.: Eerdmans, 1972). This line of argument was suggested to me by Tom D'Andrea.

83. Verhey, *Remembering Jesus*, part 5, especially pp. 413–18.

84. Robert Benne, "The Preferential Option for the Poor and American Public Policy," in Richard John Neuhaus, ed., *The Preferential Option for the Poor* (Grand Rapids, Mich.: Eerdmans, 1988), pp. 53–71.

85. The following discussion draws on Mead, *Beyond Entitlement*, chapter 3.

86. Ibid., pp. 212–15.

87. I am talking here of the popular and political perception. In reality, Social Security benefits are much higher than beneficiaries' own past contributions could finance, and Medicare involves an element of general revenue financing.

88. In a sign of the times, John Rawls eliminated any idea of "moral desert" from his influential social ethics. See *Theory of Justice*, pp. 310–15.

89. Bane and Ellwood, *Welfare Realities*, chapter 1. Aid was not conditioned on good behavior in any other sense.

90. Cullen Murphy, "Women and the Bible," *Atlantic Monthly*, August 1993, pp. 39–64; David Black, "The Calling: Contemporary Issues as well as Traditional Faith Challenge a Candidate for the Ministry," *New York Times Magazine*, May 11, 1986. In the churches I have attended, the personal attention I received was inversely proportional to how seriously these churches pursued a social mission.

91. Lawrence M. Mead, "The Politics of Disadvantage," *Society*, vol. 35, no. 5 (July/August 1998), pp. 72–76.

92. Isaiah 2:2–3; John 12:32.

93. Bonhoeffer, *Cost of Discipleship*, p. 49. He wrote, of course, well before the 1960s.

94. Sider, *Rich Christians*; U.S. House Committee on Finance, *Social Security Amendments of 1971: Hearings before the Committee on Finance on H.R. 1*, 92d Cong., 2 February 1972, pp. 2063–64.

95. Sider, *Rich Christians*, chapter 3.

96. Isaiah 40:4.

97. Dietrich Bonhoeffer, *Ethics*, ed. Eberhard Bethge, trans. Neville Horton Smith (Macmillan, 1965), pp. 62–63.

98. Robert Nozick, *Anarchy, State, and Utopia* (Basic Books, 1974).

99. Lay Commission on Catholic Social Teaching and the U.S. Economy, *Toward the Future: Catholic Social Thought and the U.S. Economy: A Lay Letter* (New York: American Catholic Committee, 1984); John Paul II, *Centisimus Annus*, section 48.

100. Charles Murray, *Losing Ground: American Social Policy, 1950–1980* (Basic Books, 1984); Marvin Olasky, *The Tragedy of American Compassion* (Wheaton, Ill.: Crossway Books, 1992).

101. Gary Burtless, "Public Spending on the Poor: Historical Trends and Economic Limits," in Danziger, Sandefur, and Weinberg, eds., *Confronting Poverty*, chapter 3.

102. Robert A. Moffitt, "Incentive Effects of the U.S. Welfare System: A Review," *Journal of Economic Literature*, vol. 30, no. 1 (March 1992), pp.1–61; and Moffit, ed., *Welfare, the Family, and Reproductive Behavior* (Washington: National Academy Press, 1998).

103. James L. Sundquist, "Has America Lost Its Social Conscience—And How Will It Get It Back?" *Political Science Quarterly*, vol. 101, no. 4 (1986), pp. 513–33.

104. Martin Gilens, *Why Americans Hate Welfare: Race, Media, and the Politics of Antipoverty Policy* (University of Chicago Press, 1999), chapters 2, 8.

105. Mead, *New Politics of Poverty*, chapters 8–9; Michael Wiseman, ed., "Research and Policy: A Symposium on the Family Support Act of 1988," *Journal of Policy Analysis and Management*, vol. 10, no. 4 (Fall 1991), pp. 588–666.

106. Gayle Hamilton and Daniel Friedlander, *Final Report on the Saturation Work Initiative Model in San Diego* (New York: Manpower Demonstration Research Corporation, November 1989); James Riccio, Daniel Friedlander, and Stephen Freedman, *GAIN: Benefits, Costs, and Three-Year Impacts of a Welfare-to-Work Program* (New York: Manpower Demonstration Research Corporation, September 1994); Gayle Hamilton and others, *National Evaluation of Welfare-to-Work Strategies: How Effective Are Different Welfare-to-Work Approaches? Five-Year Adult and Child Impacts for Eleven Programs* (New York: Manpower Demonstration Research Corporation, November 2001).

107. Mead, *New Paternalism*. Olasky, in *Tragedy of American Compassion*, chapters 1–6, emphasizes the similar element of "challenge" in the traditional charity of the nineteenth century.

108. Mead, *Beyond Entitlement*, chapters 5, 9.

109. They included Peter Edelman, Wendell Primus, and Mary Jo Bane, my coauthor on this book. Their reasons for resigning included not only PRWORA's severe work tests but other conservative features of the legislation, some of which I also opposed. See further discussion below.

110. Mead, *Beyond Entitlement*, pp. 212–15; *The New Politics of Poverty*, pp. 198–201.

111. Leo XIII, *Rerum Novarum*, section 42; John Paul II, *Laborem Exercens*, sections 16.2, 19.4–19.5. A more convincing Catholic theology of work, which does emphasize obligation, was developed by Monsignor Josemaria Escrivá, the founder of Opus Dei. See José Luis Illanes, *On the Theology of Work: Aspects of the Teaching of the Founder of Opus Dei*, trans. Michael Adams (New Rochelle, N.Y.: Scepter Press, 1982).

112. National Conference of Catholic Bishops, *Economic Justice for All*, sections 70–1, 74, 76, 188, 201, 207, 211. A preliminary draft denounced the idea that welfare recipients might be required to work for their income. There was "little or no evidence that people need to be compelled to work," the authors wrote, and assignment to unpaid jobs, or "workfare," was "a particularly objectionable requirement." See National Conference of Catholic Bishops, *First Draft—Bishops Pastoral: Catholic Social Thought and the U.S. Economy* (Washington: Origins, NC Documentary Service, November 15, 1984), section 235. The final draft deleted these comments.

113. National Conference of Catholic Bishops, *A Decade after Economic Justice for All*; Administrative Board, United States Catholic Conference, "Moral Principles and Policy Priorities for Welfare Reform" (Washington: United States Catholic Conference, August 1995).

114. David T. Ellwood, "The Impact of the Earned Income Tax Credit and Social Policy Reforms On Work, Marriage, and Living Arrangements" (Harvard University, Kennedy School of Government, November 1999).

115. U.S. Census Bureau,1994 March Current Population Survey, table 19; 2001 March Current Population Survey, table 17; March 2002 Annual Demographic Survey, table 17.

116. Rebecca M. Blank and Ron Haskins, eds., *The New World of Welfare: An Agenda for Reauthorization and Beyond* (Brookings, 2001). I have summarized the principal evidence in Mead, "Welfare Reform: Meaning and Effects," *Policy Currents*, vol. 11, no. 2 (Summer 2001), pp. 7–13.

117. Wendell Primus and others, *The Initial Impacts of Welfare Reform on the Incomes of Single-Mother Families* (Washington: Center on Budget and Policy Priorities, August 22, 1999).

118. John Paul II, *Laborem Exercens*, section 20.3.

119. Isabel V. Sawhill, "The Perils of Early Motherhood," *The Public Interest* (Winter 2002), pp. 80–83.

120. Case studies of twenty-three states by the Urban Institute and the Rockefeller Institute of Government dramatize these efforts to expand the safety net to cover the newly working poor.

121. Lawrence M. Mead, "The Politics of Conservative Welfare Reform," in Blank and Haskins, eds., *New World of Welfare*, pp. 212–17.

122. PRWORA, of which the creation of TANF was a part, also contained cuts in eligibility for a number of benefit programs. Aliens were mostly excluded from

TANF, food stamps, and SSI. The economies claimed by the law were due to these provisions, not to TANF, and additional money was invested in child care. Much of the initial upset over reform among liberals was occasioned by these eligibility cuts rather than by TANF itself.

123. I stated these views in testimony before the House Ways and Means Committee and the Senate Finance Committee in several hearings in 1995.

124. Thomas L. Gais, "Welfare Reform Findings in Brief" (Albany: State University of New York, Rockefeller Institute of Government, March 1, 2002); Malcolm L. Goggin and Deborah A. Orth, "State and County Implementation of the Family Formation and Pregnancy Prevention Goals of PRWORA" (Michigan State University, Department of Political Science, August 30, 2002).

125. U.S. Department of Health and Human Services, Administration for Children and Families, *Temporary Assistance for Needy Families Program (TANF): Fifth Annual Report to Congress* (Washington: February 2003), table 3:1:a.

126. Mead, "Welfare Reform: The Institutional Dimension."

127. States were allowed to count against their work participation targets any percent by which their caseloads had fallen since 1995. Since the caseload fall was unexpectedly great, this reduced the work targets below a level that would have forced most states to build work requirements fully into welfare programs.

128. U.S. Department of Health and Human Services, Administration for Children and Families, *Working toward Independence* (Washington: February 26, 2002).

129. "Will Tinkering Bring the Building Down?" *Economist*, March 2, 2002, pp. 29–30; Robin Toner, "Rallies in Capital Protest Bush Welfare Proposals," *New York Times*, March 6, 2002, p. A17.

130. I base this on written statements by several church groups that I acquired at a hearing on reauthorization before the House Ways and Means Committee, April 11, 2002. These groups included the National Conference of Catholic Bishops, the National Council of the Churches of Christ in the USA, the Unitarian Universalist Service Committee, the Evangelical Lutheran Church in America, and the United Church of Christ.

131. If an adult recipient declines to cooperate with the work test, states can remove this person from the grant but continue aid for the rest of the family, in what is called a partial sanction. I would require a full-family sanction, or ending the entire cash grant. The family, however, would still be eligible for food stamps and health benefits.

132. I testified along these lines in hearings on reauthorization before the House Ways and Means Committee and the Senate Finance Committee in April 2002. For a summary, see Lawrence M. Mead, "Rebuilding Welfare into a Work-Based System," *Poverty Research News* (Northwestern University, Joint Center for Poverty Research), vol. 5, no. 6 (November–December 2001), pp. 8–9.

A REPLY TO MEAD

MARY JO BANE

LARRY MEAD AND I have had a long-running dialogue on welfare and welfare reform, agreeing on many issues, respectfully disagreeing on others. I have especially admired Larry's attention over the years to program implementation and management, and I share his view that the ways in which programs are operated and benefits delivered crucially shape their effects.

I have come to appreciate another dimension of Larry's approach to social policy, which I also share: a belief in the importance of the Christian commitments that inevitably, but up to now implicitly, have shaped our personal and political response to the poor. I am grateful for the opportunity to carry our conversation into this other dimension. In this response, I will identify and explore three areas in which Larry and I disagree, though perhaps not as much as our readers might have expected: our interpretation of the Christian story; our articulation of the problem of poverty; and our policy recommendations on entitlements and work requirements.

The Christian Story

For two policy analysts to argue over theological interpretation certainly is both unusual and presumptuous, given that whole disciplines devote themselves to moral theology and its scriptural and rational roots. On the other hand, moral theologians often make empirical claims—many times, from my point of view, in a quite unsophisticated way. Nonetheless, they recognize that the terrain claimed by social scientists is indeed relevant to their attempts to translate theology into practical terms.[1] Social scientists have been much less willing to venture into theological or even philosophical territory in their policy analyses, thus ignoring the moral underpinnings of policy discussion. Ideally, no doubt, all of us would be fully trained and sophisticated in both sets of disciplines and capable of genuinely collaborative work. But until that happens, we will come to the other discipline as amateurs. For most of us who take our religious commitments seriously in our private and public lives, our theology is both nonprofessional and unarticulated. But it is a step toward fuller understanding to attempt to articulate what we believe and what we are committed to. So perhaps an attempt to engage and clarify our amateur theologies may be useful to others who have not been so foolhardy as to venture into this territory—and perhaps it may encourage them to do so.

As a Catholic, I am part of a tradition that has always seen the community rather than the individual as the repository of moral insights and that has always seen Scripture as one among several sources of moral guidance.[2] This tradition has not always been constructive: for many centuries, for example, lay Catholics were discouraged from reading the Bible as individuals, lest they misinterpret it; instead the Bible was presented to them, in properly interpreted short segments, in the liturgy. The bishops of the church also reserved to themselves the tasks of discerning and teaching morality, only in the last forty years recognizing in some instances the important role of individual conscience. But although the teaching office of the church (the magisterium) sometimes has been stifling and out of touch, it does provide a rich tradition of thought that has developed over centuries and has been articulated in a number of papal and episcopal documents.

I read and pray with Scripture myself, as I infer that Larry does, and I read and am sympathetic to many of the writings of liberation theologians, but I also take seriously and attempt to present fairly the social teachings of the Catholic Church. My reading of the social teachings of the church, with their sources in tradition, reason, and experience as well as Scripture, lies behind some of my agreements and disagreements with Larry's reading of Scripture. We agree on the important themes of community and responsibility. We disagree on the extent to which the gospels tell a story of a preference for the poor, and we also disagree on the extent to which the Jesus of the gospels expected or required reciprocity.

There is always the danger of selecting Scripture texts to suit one's own purposes, and dueling with proof-texts is not a particularly edifying activity. That is why placing Scripture within a centuries-long tradition of discernment and dialogue within the church can act as a check on individual prejudices. And it does seem to me that reading the gospel within that tradition has rightly led the church to conclude that Jesus' announcement of his mission as "bringing good news to the poor"[3] indeed framed and shaped his whole public life. Jesus spent his life among the poor, and he had stinging words of rebuke for the rich and powerful of his time. The church teaches that although Jesus deeply loved all men and women, he had a special place in his heart for the poor and vulnerable. We are told, "Go and do likewise."[4]

The church also has concluded, as it has read the gospels over the centuries, that Jesus meant what he said about forgiveness and generosity in the Sermon on the Mount and that those radical themes characterized his whole life, his whole teaching, and his death. Jesus did not make God's love, forgiveness, and healing contingent on good behavior but extended it graciously and generously to sinners, to outcasts, and to enemies. Again, we are told, "Go and do likewise."

This reading of Scripture and church teaching is reinforced by what I have called the Catholic sensibility—intuitions about and responses to people and the world that are shaped by our sacramental imagination, liturgy, and prayer. Catholicism at its best is joyful, hopeful, inclusive, and generous. These virtues can of course give rise to foolish optimism, wishful thinking, undisciplined appetites, and permissiveness. Larry seems to me to be more of a Calvinist in the best sense of that tradition: disciplined, responsible, skeptical about human nature, and critical of human behavior. These virtues can give rise to (though I have not seen these in Larry) meanness, exclusivity, and unforgiving judgment.

Because of our somewhat different readings of the Scriptures and these different sensibilities, rooted, I believe, in our religious outlooks (and perhaps our personalities!), Larry and I tend to err on different sides in situations of uncertainty. These tendencies may be as important as our differences in regard to empirical interpretations and predictions in explaining why we come to different conclusions on some policy issues.

Scope and Explanations of the Problem

A second area in which Larry and I differ has to do with the definition of poverty and explanations of the problem. Larry focuses his attention on working-age adults who do not work, arguing that this group has been the center of most policy debate and dissension over the last few decades. He also argues that nonworking adults are the predominant group among the poor, that nonwork is the reason for their poverty, and that their not working results from cultural features rather than from the absence of opportunities. This analysis leads Larry, logically and single-mindedly, to focus his policy attention on the issue of work requirements in welfare programs. I frame the problem more broadly and see a broader set of explanations, and in the course of doing that, I raise a broader set of policy issues to which we must attend. I focus first on the empirical questions on which Larry and I differ, acknowledging that our reading of the empirical evidence may be influenced by our values and sensibilities. Next I take up our policy disagreements, which of course derive from disagreements about both empirical evidence and values.

My framing of the broader problem is largely a matter of simple numbers. In 2001, according to the Census Bureau, 32.9 million Americans fell below the official income poverty line. Of those, 9.6 million were adults between the ages of eighteen and sixty-four who did not work during the year. Only 800,000 were eighteen- to sixty-four-year-old female heads of household with children who did not work during the year and who gave their reasons for not working as something other than sickness or disability; these women represent the population of major concern in the welfare reform debates.[5] By my calculation, they represent 2 percent of the poor. I believe we should be concerned about the other 98 percent as well.

Now let me quickly qualify that overstatement. Probably the fairest way to establish the number of nonworking, nonelderly poor is to include all nonworking poor unrelated individuals and nonworking family heads plus their families. My best estimate of that number is 14.1 million, or 43 percent of the poor.[6] But that still leaves 57 percent of the poor who are elderly or working or who belong to families in which the head of household works. For these poor, work requirements in welfare programs cannot be the only policy issue of interest.

Of course, Larry and I agree that the Census Bureau definition of income poverty is not the only and probably not the best way to identify the population that public policy ought to be concerned about. One approach to redefinition would narrow it to look at the long-term poor who live in poor urban neighborhoods. This redefinition would raise the proportion of nonworking female heads in the population of concern, to be sure, but it also would lower the absolute numbers by a good deal.[7] And I would argue that it does not preclude alternative explanations for their situations that work requirements do not speak to.

Another approach to redefinition would look at social exclusion instead of or in addition to income poverty. This approach emphasizes the importance of work and of civic and political participation to human flourishing in this society. It leads us to look at both lack of personal capability at the individual level and lack of opportunity at the societal level—for example, social exclusion resulting from lack of the cognitive skills or education necessary to participate in society; from physical or emotional disabilities; or from lack of access to decent work and opportunities for civic and political participation. A related approach would consider educational and health deprivations as worthy of concern in their own right.[8] Either of these reformulations invites us to look broadly at both explanations and policy responses.

I settled, as for the most part Larry did as well, for looking at those defined as poor by the Census Bureau income poverty measure, pointing out that they are a very diverse group indeed along a number of dimensions, including but not limited to work status. I highlighted the disproportionate representation among the poor of African Americans, Hispanics, and immigrants and discussed explanations for and responses to their special situations. In my discussion of income transfer programs I looked at other programs as well as at AFDC/TANF, recognizing that there are groups other than single parents among the poor whose needs ought to be of concern for policymakers.

I do not disagree with Larry that the program conventionally referred to as welfare—that is, TANF—and its predominant clientele, nonworking single-parent families, has generated the most policy controversy and concern. But I do disagree that we ought therefore to continue to focus solely on that program and group when we talk about poverty. They are a minority of those we ought to be concerned about, however broadly or narrowly we define poverty, and we ought to recognize that.

My broader definition of the problem leads me to focus on three areas of concern that Larry considers less important: racial stigma, immigration, and the availability of jobs. I will not repeat my discussion of racial differences and possible explanations for them, except to note a few points. The racial disparities in all areas of disadvantage—including income but also educational attainment, health status, and other measures of capability deprivation and social exclusion—are striking. Larry and I agree that simple discrimination of the old-fashioned sort cannot explain current racial disparities. I, however, find Glenn Loury's analysis of racial stigma a persuasive alternative to cultural explanations that are less historically and psychologically sensitive.[9] If racial stigma and discrimination continue to characterize race relations in this country, as Loury argues, then any approach to poverty must also be concerned with expanding opportunities in ways that attend to and attempt to overcome the effects of racial stigma.

Likewise, any approach to poverty must recognize the fact of immigration, which is bringing about dramatic changes in the demography of this country and creating spillover effects in other areas as well. Immigrants make up a substantial minority of the poor, and their poverty rates are disproportionately high. That is not necessarily a problem of great concern if immigrant poverty represents a first-generation phenomenon resulting from less skilled immigrants making their way into the American mainstream from countries where they were much worse off. A serious problem does arise, however, if, as some studies suggest, the second and third generations of immigrants come to be locked into the same patterns of racial stigma and cultural disadvantage that have long plagued African Americans.[10] It would seem sensible to prevent this at the onset, with special attention to the health and education needs of the children of immigrants and to overcoming any emerging discrimination in employment and housing that leads to cultural segregation.

My disagreement with Larry about the importance of job stimulation is of a different sort. Despite my argument above that nonwork is not the only problem that policymakers should be concerned with and that non-working single parents are a small part of the poverty problem, Larry and I agree on the importance of employment in poverty policy. Our agreement on this is worth emphasizing. It comes from our shared sense that income is not the only dimension of poverty and that participation in the social, economic, and political life of society is a crucial aspect of human flourishing and thus a crucial goal for public policy. We both read the gospels in a way that emphasizes Jesus' mission of restoring outcasts to full membership in the community, which includes taking responsibility for self and others. Neither of us is satisfied with poverty policies that simply transfer income and do not attend to work.

Larry and I also agree that many past government efforts to ensure employment opportunities by providing jobs have been failures. I suspect we agree that the socialist states failed spectacularly, that the Depression-era works programs in this country mostly succeeded, and that government job creation of the CETA variety often, though not always, was inefficient and occasionally corrupt. Where we may disagree is in our willingness to consider the necessity for and possible effectiveness of newer approaches to stimulating jobs: new versions of job credits, government-stimulated private economic development in poor areas, and so on.

Our disagreements here may be an example of what I labeled earlier as our tendency to err on different sides in conditions of uncertainty. We genuinely do not know the extent to which people currently out of work could get jobs if they really tried and were willing to accept situations that were less than perfect. I am inclined to give people the benefit of the doubt and argue that in some locations and some situations nonwork results from lack of jobs rather than lack of effort; Larry is stricter. Similarly, the evidence is mixed on the extent to which various approaches to job stimulation are efficient and effective. I am inclined to give them a try; Larry seems to be more skeptical. My approach runs the risk of wasting taxpayers' money on programs that are not needed or do not work; Larry's approach runs the risk of denying productive opportunities to people who need and would take advantage of them. It is perhaps a stretch to link these different approaches to the different sensibilities of our religious traditions, but I am inclined to give that a try as well.

Entitlement and Reciprocity

Larry outlines three approaches to poverty policy: entitlement, self-reliance, and reciprocity. I agree with his rejection of self-reliance as the sole approach to poverty policy. I disagree with his rejection of entitlements.

Larry distinguishes entitlements from social insurance, seeing the programs of the Social Security system as examples of reciprocity. He does not in his opening essay discuss Supplemental Security Income, the other major cash assistance program for the elderly and disabled, but he might make the argument, as many do, that entitlements without work requirements for those who are unable to work are appropriate.

I want to make a broader argument—an argument for entitlement to basic levels of assistance that encompasses the working-age population even when they do not work. To examine the questions of who is entitled to what and under what conditions, I will focus on the food stamp program and also discuss shelter and medical care.

My moral argument asserts that the community is obligated to provide basic levels of sustenance, health care, and education for all its members. That obligation is based on the preciousness of every human being and on the belief that God's plan desires the flourishing of every person. It assumes the obligation of all to contribute to the community but puts a special burden on the rich. And in the Christian tradition, the obligation to care for the neighbor in need is not contingent on the worthiness or behavior of the neighbor. That is the crux, I believe, of the Sermon on the Mount and the parable of the Good Samaritan, which are central to the gospels and to the church's general insistence on compassion and care for the poor. As noted above, this general obligation to the poor is central to my reading of Scripture, but not to Larry's. Here our religious traditions do put us in different places.

The Scriptures, of course, do not enlighten us much on the questions of who is obligated to provide what for whom under what conditions. The Christian ideal, lived out in the early Christian communities described (or idealized) in the Acts of the Apostles and in many religious orders, is of common ownership and equal sharing. Christians seeking perfection embrace voluntary poverty and follow St. Francis of Assisi in giving to the poor, presumably to the point that all share equally in the goods of both divine and human creation. But the church has long seen this approach as a counsel of perfection, not a requirement to be imposed on all. And it has recognized the value of private ownership and market exchange as sensible responses to human nature, which is less than perfect.[11]

Nonetheless, the church continues to emphasize the obligation to provide for the least advantaged, not just as a matter for private charity but also as a requirement of justice and thus an appropriate task for government. I suggest that this obligation implies the articulation and implementation of entitlements to basic levels of food, shelter, health care, and education. I suspect that Larry and I do not disagree about the appropriateness, certainly in this country and even in very poor countries, of free and equal primary and secondary education available to all. We may well disagree about food, shelter, and medical care, so I will begin with the food stamp program as an example for exploring our differences.

Assistance to the poor, I contend (and I suspect Larry agrees), should respect the basic dignity and full membership in the community of all. At the same time, it should encourage and expect responsibility and contributions to the community and discourage free-riders. And it should do all this humanely and efficiently.

The food stamp program, as I explained in my opening essay, is an uneasy but I believe basically sensible compromise for meeting these criteria.[12] Food stamps are not contingent on worthiness: they are available to old and young, the sick and the healthy, individuals and families, alcoholics and teetotalers, workers and nonworkers. Eligibility for food stamps is with some exceptions determined only by need defined as low income. That expresses our society's belief—correct, I believe—that no one in this society ought to go hungry.

The uneasiness of the compromise comes in some of the features of the food stamp program: it is an in-kind program, with guarantee levels that are quite low, sufficient only to purchase a frugal nutritious diet.[13] Aid is given in a form that can be used only for food and that identifies users as recipients of public benefits. The application procedure for the program is intrusive and intimidating. All these features signal societal disapproval and deter most of those who do not need aid and some of those who do from taking advantage of the program.

One question about the food stamp compromise is whether society's different goals are best met by meal programs, commodity distribution, food vouchers, or cash. Feeding programs—for example, free or cheap meals provided at community centers or shelters—tend to rely on inconvenience and stigma as ways of discouraging free-riders. Their usual location in poor neighborhoods has the same effect. Commodity distribution programs also rely on inconvenience, stigma, and limited choice; they may enforce income eligibility standards as well. Food voucher and cash programs tend to impose income eligibility standards enforced through fairly elaborate application procedures. Food vouchers involve more stigma and limit choice more than cash does. Any of the models may incorporate work requirements.

The U.S. choice of a food voucher model seems to me to be a reasonable compromise in balancing goals: it involves some stigma and inconvenience, but less than meals or commodity distribution programs do; it has eligibility standards but fewer requirements than one might demand in a cash program. I do not believe that there is any excuse in administering any of these programs for demeaning recipients, but it is reasonable to use a humane application procedure as a screening device and also to use vouchers rather than cash as a way of ensuring that program benefits go to those who lack food.

The relatively low level of food stamp benefits is also, to my mind, a reasonable compromise. They are meant to provide an adequate but frugal level of nutrition and certainly are not overly generous in meeting that standard. But then they also are made available to pretty much everybody, not limited, as other programs are, to the elderly and disabled or to children and their caretakers.

In this framework, one can ask whether adding real, enforced work requirements to the food stamp program would improve its basic balancing act between providing for the needy and encouraging responsibility. Support and encouragement for employment certainly are appropriate. Going beyond that to requiring work for food is certainly not an unknown concept in international relief work and domestic charity.[14] In some international programs the work is provided; the willingness to show up and contribute to a construction project or service effort is then compensated with food. In many settings this is an entirely sensible approach, increasing production, building skills, and deterring free-riders all at once.

However, I tend to think that in the American food stamp program, real work requirements would tilt an already uneasy balance too much in the direction of deterrence. It would be entirely impractical to provide government-funded and -supervised work settings for millions of food stamp recipients; in this country, the cost of providing the work would almost certainly exceed the modest cost of the benefits. Work requirements would more likely take the form of a required number of applications for employment that would need to be documented as a condition of eligibility; this would likely hurt disproportionately those who are most disorganized, least functional, and thus arguably most needy. For practical as well as humane reasons, therefore, I would oppose serious work requirements in the food stamp program and support its continuation and indeed expansion as an entitlement.

The logic of the argument that I have just laid out for food stamps would seem to extend as well to other necessities of life, for example, clothing and shelter. The gospels certainly call Christians to quite radical generosity and imply that the neighbor in need, simply by virtue of his or her need, ought, in the language of Matthew 25, be fed, given drink, taken in, given clothing, and visited when sick or in prison. The question for a democratic polity is whether and to what extent the mandate for sharing goods with the needy translates into tax-funded entitlement programs.

Although I believe that Christian communities are called to a generosity as radical and as nonjudgmental as that of Jesus, polities are rightly focused on justice and concerned with efficiency and productivity as well as compassion. This society has worked out the balancing of its concerns in a relatively sensible approach to guaranteeing food for the hungry. There is less consensus on the issues of housing for the homeless or health care for the sick. Some states and municipalities provide minimal shelters and most guarantee emergency care for the sick, but there is no entitlement to housing or to health care.

This is a failing of our very rich society, I believe. Surely we ought to be able to provide basic levels of shelter and health care to everyone, constructing programs analogous to the food stamp program that are affordable and that avoid serious incentive problems. Though in the current political environment such sentiments may seem hopelessly utopian, I believe we ought to move in that direction and do so without being overly concerned with reciprocity.

This is not to deny the importance of the values of inclusion, participation, and contribution or to argue against providing encouragement and opportunities for work whenever possible. And as I have argued, requiring work for cash from adults who are able to work in programs like TANF is quite appropriate. The basic difference between my stance and Larry's is that I would provide a basic level of food, shelter, and medical care for everyone, even those who fail to live up to the expectations of reciprocity that we rightly build into government programs. I believe that this is required by both Christian morality and the norms of our national social contract.

I readily concede that an approach that provides for basic needs is likely to lead to some inefficiencies and that some people may take advantage of the system. I wish that this were not so, but it is. Nonetheless, my Catholic sensibility leads me to err on the side of generosity, giving others the benefit of the doubt—and to err unashamedly.

Notes

1. Two moral theologians who do make good use of empirical data are David Hollenbach and Thomas Massaro. See, for example Hollenbach, *The Common Good and Christian Ethics* (Cambridge University Press, 2002) and Massaro, *Catholic Social Teaching and United States Welfare Reform* (Collegeville, Minn.: Liturgical Press, 1998).

2. A good statement of the Catholic stance toward moral theology appears in Richard M. Gula, *Reason Informed by Faith: Foundations of Catholic Morality* (Mahwah, N.J.: Paulist Press, 1989).

3. Luke 4:18.

4. "Go and do likewise" is the closing line of the parable of the Good Samaritan, Luke 10:25–37.

5. Poverty numbers are from the Current Population Survey, conducted by the U.S. Bureau of the Census. Some of the data are reported in U.S. Bureau of the

Census, *Poverty in the United States: 2001*, Current Population Reports, P60-219 (2002). Additional data are available through the Census Bureau at http://ferret. bls.census.gov/macro/032002/ pov/toc.htm [March 31, 2003]. The employment data are in table 10.

6. Table 10 reports 3.978 million nonworking poor unrelated individuals and 2.744 million nonworking poor family heads. Average family size for poor families is 3.4 persons. Assuming that nonworking poor families are the same average size as all poor families would mean that there were 14.125 million poor individuals in the families of nonworking heads. Table 10 also reported 3.293 million nonworking poor elderly, which would bring the total number of nonworking poor to 17.418 million, or 53 percent of the poor (http://ferret.bls.census.gov/macro/ 032002/ pov/toc.htm [March 31, 2003]).

7. Paul Jargowsky, in *Poverty and Place: Ghettos, Barrios, and the American City* (New York: Russell Sage Foundation, 1997) estimated that 18 percent of the poor in 1990 lived in high-poverty areas, defined as census tracts with poverty rates greater than 40 percent. Unpublished recent work by Jargowsky suggests that this number went down substantially between 1990 and 2000. Of the adults living in high-poverty neighborhoods in 1990, 54 percent were women, 64 percent of whom were not working (p. 96).

8. The notion of poverty as capability deprivation is developed in Amartya Sen, *Development as Freedom* (New York: Anchor Books, 1999). Social exclusion is a more European concept that is developed in a number of works, including a collection in which the concept is applied to the United States: Alfred J. Kahn and Sheila B. Kamerman, eds., *Beyond Child Poverty: The Social Exclusion of Children* (Columbia University, Institute for Child and Family Poverty, 2002).

9. Glenn C. Loury, *The Anatomy of Racial Inequality* (Harvard University Press, 2002).

10. See, for example, Carola Suarez-Orozco and Marcelo Suarez-Orozco, *Children of Immigrants* (Harvard University Press, 2001).

11. See, for example, John Paul II, Centesimus Annus: *On the Hundredth Anniversary of* Rerum Novarum, in David J. O'Brien and Thomas A. Shannon, eds., *Catholic Social Thought* (Maryknoll, N.Y.: Orbis Books, 1991), pp. 439–88.

12. Detailed information on the food stamp program can be found on the website of the Department of Agriculture (www.fns.usda.gov/fsp/ [March 31, 2003]).

13. For example, the maximum food stamp allotment in 2002 was $465 per month for a household of four.

14. The various approaches used in different countries and the arguments supporting them are laid out well in K. Subbarao and others, *Safety Net Programs and Poverty Reeducation* (Washington: World Bank, 1997).

A REPLY TO BANE

LAWRENCE M. MEAD

IT IS AN honor to respond to Mary Jo Bane's Catholic approach to poverty. She is an eminent researcher. Her work has done much to define the problems of poverty and dependency that national policy strives to solve.[1] And, unusual for an academic, she also has actually administered welfare programs at the state and national level. I have learned much from hands-on contact with government myself, so I accord her views unusual authority. I also respect her for her decision to resign from the Clinton administration over the 1996 welfare reform act. I took a more favorable view of that law. But her action served something more important—the civic values of American government. To sacrifice a valued position on an issue of principle honors the essence of public service, which is to place the public interest above one's own.

We disagree less than one might expect. We share the belief that an ambitious national antipoverty policy is necessary. Mary Jo now claims to support the general direction of our national policy, as I do. But we disagree about much of the rationale for this policy and about some details. These differences are revealing. Much of Mary Jo's policy position is moderate and realistic. But I find her position difficult to reconcile with her theology, which relies chiefly on traditional Catholic social teaching.

The Nature of Poverty

In her analysis of the social problem, Mary Jo holds to a moderate version of what I call sociologism—the attribution of poverty and dependency to barriers of opportunity outside the poor themselves. She sees poverty as "the deprivation of the societal structures and personal opportunities to live out God's plan." As I explain in my opening essay, external social conditions do not explain well why people remain poor for any length of time in the United States in recent decades, at least among those of working age or their children.

For the most part, working-aged poverty is due in the first instance to single parenthood and nonwork by the parents of children, both mothers and fathers. Those patterns, in turn, are not obviously driven by outside adversities such as racial discrimination or a scarcity of jobs. Indeed, they were far rarer under Jim Crow and during the Depression than they are today, when social conditions are far more favorable to the poor. Social barriers have much more to do, I believe, with the highly unequal incomes found among working Americans and their families, few of whom are poor. In short, barriers explain inequality better than they do poverty.

It is true that many of the long-term poor believe that they are fenced in by barriers. Ask poor parents why they are in trouble, and they will mention lack of jobs or child care, disability, terrible schooling, unfair employers, the unjust incarceration of a spouse, and so on. In many cases, the reasons are valid. But experience has proven that to adopt the social analysis of the poor themselves generally is not a help to them. Merely pushing back the barriers by adding some new benefit—for example, by guaranteeing child care or training for better jobs—prompts few of those served actually to go to work. Some new impediment usually arises to postpone actually seeking and taking a job. In the end, the belief in barriers reflects a defeatist culture of poverty, in which people want to work and otherwise observe middle-class mores, but prove unable to do so in practice. This culture I find to be the chief cause of poverty. Programs that help people without expecting anything of them ratify that culture and so become part of the problem.[2]

Interestingly, both I and Mary Jo seized on Amartya Sen's concept of capability as an attractive vision of what overcoming poverty might mean.

The goal, Bane says, is to ensure that everyone has the personal "capabilities necessary for human flourishing"; the poor, then, are those who are "deprived of these basic capabilities." But precisely because capability connotes something internal to the person, it is unclear how anything external can explain its presence or absence. In principle, society could overcome income poverty simply by giving money to the poor. But how can it ensure that everyone has these basic capacities? Sen was thinking of the absence of education or health care for much of the poor in the third world, but in the United States, the vast majority of the poor already have these benefits. What is much more lacking is the personal organization needed to make good use of the opportunities already offered by the world's most open and affluent society—especially the self-discipline to get through school, obey the law, work steadily, and avoid trouble in one's personal life.

Ensuring these capabilities is not principally a matter of social generosity. The plain truth is, nobody knows how to do it. We know that most children who are brought up in functioning, two-parent families emerge from home able to get through school, avoid the police, and become employed before becoming parents. But we do not know how to correct the deficits of the children who fail to do these things, many of them from poor, single-parent families. Merely to offer benefits or services achieves little. The best programs employ what I call paternalism. They link benefits with direction, obligating their recipients to behave in constructive ways—such as by working or staying in school—in return for help. That combination mimics the care and attention that the clients should have had from their parents, had their families been stronger. But even these programs have a much smaller impact on skills than we would wish.

I also find sociologism alien to the Bible. The effect of it is to treat the poor as victims and pass all the responsibility for change to society. In fact, the case for structural injustice was a lot stronger in biblical times than in ours. The rich were understood to be not simply people with high incomes but those who had acquired riches in some unjust way, such as by allying with the Romans or becoming tax collectors. Wealth was conferred on dependents by patrons, who were part of an unjust power structure.[3] In the United States, which has an entirely different economy, the open market usually forces the rich to serve the wider society in order to amass their wealth. Most of them are no longer exploiters.[4]

But despite the injustices of their time, neither Jesus nor the prophets call for social reform in the impersonal, modern sense of changing the social structure. Rather, they criticize the rich and powerful as individuals. They call on them to be more attentive to the poor. But they do not tell them precisely what to do. They utter no mandate to abolish poverty or reduce inequality in the economic sense that we emphasize today. Nor do they exempt those who are not rich from responsibility for their own lives. The laws of good behavior remain in force for both rich and poor. The solution to social problems is seen to lie in greater fidelity to God's will by the entire society. Changes in policy or in institutions are secondary.

RACE

In a sociological analysis, the most important barrier to economic equality is race. Clergy and seminary faculty, I have found, tend particularly to believe that racial discrimination against blacks is the master cause of poverty and inequality in the United States. Most scholars of poverty, however, give it less weight. Among the poor, every race is well represented. The same is true among the scholars and policymakers who fight poverty. The social problems of poor blacks do not seem distinctive. While most of the poor are nonwhite, race per se is seldom an important cause of poverty once one has allowed for its first-order causes, particularly nonwork and unwed parenthood. To make a case for race, one has to show that it is a special cause of these behaviors. Either blacks are especially prone to these patterns or they are driven into them by a hostile society.

As I mention in my opening essay, the evidence does not support the idea that the economy denies blacks all employment. To the contrary, huge numbers of blacks have been hired off welfare in recent years by employers hungry for labor. The case for barriers is stronger in regard to wages and inequality among the employed. Black workers typically make less than whites, but this is due largely to their having lower skills and poorer educations than average, not directly to racial bias. The evidence for discrimination in housing is a good deal stronger. But because housing patterns have little to do with whether blacks are employed, it is hard to see residential segregation as a major cause of poverty. The inner-city ghetto concentrates poor blacks together, but it has little to do with why they are poor in the first place. Family and employment problems are much more central.[5]

The case that blacks are especially prone to dysfunctional behavior is weak in the areas of employment and education. Work levels for blacks run close to those for whites, either on or off welfare, and among the poor and nonpoor. Blacks do less well than other races in school, but over time their progress has been impressive. In quantity of education, if not quality, they have largely closed the gap with whites. In part due to education gains, a large black professional class has emerged since the civil rights era. These facts make me doubt theories that blacks are innately less intelligent than whites, although on average they score lower on standard intelligence tests.

The case that blacks are prone to dysfunction is stronger for crime and unwed childbearing, especially when viewing the race as a whole. In the United States, almost as many blacks are jailed as whites, even though blacks represent only 13 percent of the population, and 69 percent of black births occur out of wedlock, compared with 27 percent for whites.[6] Relations among black men and women appear to be deeply troubled. At all incomes, many fewer blacks than whites manage to form stable marriages, although rates of divorce and single parenthood have risen sharply for both races. A weak family also is found in some black areas outside the United States, such as in the Caribbean. These patterns seem rooted in the historical background of blacks, both in this country and in Africa.[7] Overcoming them will require a long struggle by blacks themselves—including the black church—as well as the larger society.

Mary Jo cites approvingly Glenn Loury's ingenious theory of racial inequality. Loury argues that exaggerated ideas of ghetto social problems causes whites to minimize contact with blacks, making it more likely that the impressions they do gain of blacks will be negative. Blacks for their part are more liable to behave destructively because of the belief that white society will never accept them. While there is truth to this, it is not the largest truth. Information problems may cause whites to exaggerate black problems, but not to invent them. Differences between white and black lifestyles are real and substantial, especially in the areas of crime and family life. Until they subside, trust among the races will remain difficult.

Neither Loury nor anyone else has explained the core mystery of black poverty, which is its dysfunctional character. If high levels of crime and unwed childbearing were an effective response to white mistreatment, they could be viewed as sensible, even admirable. In fact, they harm blacks themselves much more than whites. They are much in contrast with the highly effective actions that blacks took, both individually and collectively, to advance themselves in the decades between emancipation and civil rights. For the black middle class, efforts to get educated, get a good job, and get ahead continue unabated, and they continue to bear fruit. Social policy toward poor blacks aims largely to persuade them to adopt the same strategy.

But to repeat, in explaining *poverty*, race counts for less than in explaining overall racial inequality. The undiscipline seen among the black poor is also seen among the poor of other races. As many have noted, a century ago the Irish poor had the same reputation for unreliability found among the black poor today. That famous black sense of being held hostage to the larger society is less distinctive than we think. What is it but the culture of poverty, which afflicts the poor of all races? Far from race producing poverty, poverty really helps produce race, in the sense of today's racial problem. Overcoming poverty and its lifestyle is not an endeavor that we need to understand in racial terms. But if we succeed in it, we also will do much to promote racial integration.

THE RESPONSE TO POVERTY

Mary Jo would have society respond to poverty primarily through support and acceptance of the poor. The Catholic tradition stresses the "equal dignity of all." It also asserts a "preferential option" for the poor, meaning that it "privileges the experience and aspirations of those uniquely precious men and women whom we categorize as poor." I think these positions get in the way of a realistic social policy. If we construe the poor only as precious and vulnerable, then we cannot confront the elements in their lifestyle that help to create poverty today.

In a democratic society where most people have to work, employment should be seen as *essential* to dignity rather than a threat to it. Do we enhance dignity most by exempting people from the common social expectations—or by enforcing them? Provided the demands are reasonable and common, I think the latter.[8] As I explain in my opening essay, the idea of a preference for the poor, in today's sense of those of low income, also seems to me to run counter to the gospels, where we see Jesus caring for people in all stations of life.

Catholic social teaching, as expressed by the popes and the American bishops, expects responsibility from the poor as well as from society. Mary Jo endorses that principle. But in the official texts, the demands on the poor remain largely rhetorical. All the specific injunctions to provide for the poor are laid on government. In practice, deliverance from need is understood mostly as something that society can give to the poor by an act of magnanimity, not something to which those aided must also contribute. The popes and the bishops specifically forbid the policy of requiring welfare mothers to work that the government is now enforcing, although it is successful by virtually every measure.

Interpreted in this permissive way, the biblical tradition unwittingly abets the general redistribution of responsibility away from the poor and other out groups that has occurred since the 1960s. In any public setting, it is difficult to hold the needy and members of racial minorities—and, to a lesser extent, women—responsible for themselves, because opinion leaders, including elected officials, have defined these groups as victims of whom nothing can be expected. The burden of responding to their complaints was shifted to society and especially to white men. The latter were bound in new ways, such as affirmative action, so that others might be freed. This psychic class system, where "rich" and "poor" face different moral expectations, now crosscuts the traditional class system, rooted in the economy. Some people were privileged in one order, some in the other, some in both, and some—including most white men—in neither.

Public resistance to the system goes far to explain the conservative backlash that hit American politics after 1980. But although most conservatives oppose the moral privileges granted the favored groups, they have not yet broken the grip of psychic class on many politicians, the universities, most of the nonprofit world, and most leading national media. Conservatives have opposed liberal government, but mainly in the name of less government. They have not yet restored a more civic regime, in which minimal civilities are expected without question of every race, gender, and class. Since an effective antipoverty policy requires demanding some things from the poor as well as helping them, one of its good side effects is to combat moral inequality.

The original author of the Catholic approach, Mary Jo says, is "a compassionate, inclusive, peaceful Jesus—who loved, healed, and forgave indiscriminately." This passive and accepting image is cherished by the liberal church, Catholic and Protestant alike. The Jesus I see in the gospels is a more dynamic and demanding figure and a less predictable one. He is indeed loving and accepting of the outcast, but he is also demanding, of rich and poor alike. He reacts in unexpected ways to people, embracing some but challenging others. Sometimes he does both at once, as with the rich young man whom he loves for his fidelity to the law—but then tells to give everything he has to the poor and come follow him.[9]

George Lakoff says that two images of the family are at war in American culture. In the "nurturant parent" conception, parents offer limitless support to their children, setting behavioral standards mainly by their own example. In the "strict father" model, in contrast, children are held to rigid standards of conduct, the better to make them self-reliant. The two visions inspire opposed approaches to social policy, one stressing succor for the vulnerable, the other morality for the wayward.[10] The Catholic tradition, as Mary Jo presents it, endorses almost entirely the first of these models. But the Jesus we see in the gospels expresses both. He is generous and demanding in equal measure. Indeed, he transcends the duality. He embraces the poor, but he also thinks they need God's laws. To him, the laws are "More to be desired . . . than gold, even much fine gold."[11]

The Catholic conception misses the element of challenge in the life of following Jesus. Mary Jo notes that Jesus healed people so that they could once again participate in the community, but in her account there is no clear requirement that they do so. The gospels, in contrast, summon Jesus' disciples to a strenuous life. The parable of the pounds dramatizes that God calls even those with the smallest gifts and the humblest callings to make of them everything that they can.[12] Doing so takes qualities that are not meek and mild. As John Schneider writes:

The essence of life is not in the quantity and visibility of our domin-
ion, but in its quality. This only [God] truly knows and judges, and
he will reward our labors as only he can. By his grace there is eternal glory buried within the passing smallness of our lives. The
teacher, the doctor, the lawyer, the insurance salesperson, the small
motel manager, the fry cook, the owner of the toy store, the professional athlete, the school janitor, the film actor, the hardware mer-
chant, the corporate executive, the college administrator—great or
small—all have pounds to trade with royal grace, purpose, and
effect. Such servants befit the warrior and king of the universe
whom they serve.[13]

The Catholic Sensibility

Mary Jo mentions a "Catholic sensibility," meaning a general view of the
world rather than a specific doctrine. It embodies the attitudes already
mentioned above but goes beyond them. It "experiences God in community" and sees the world as "a hopeful place that is basically good and in
which redemption is always possible." Other elements of this outlook
include a proclivity to balance competing values, to assert both individual
and collective responsibility for social problems (at least in principle), to
affirm both public and private property, and to assert the principle of "subsidiarity." The latter holds that social problems such as poverty should be
dealt with as close to the local level as possible, ideally by the individual
who is poor, then by the family or neighborhood, then by community
organizations, and then by the government—preferably local rather than
national. These attitudes permeate the papal encyclicals and the statements of the American bishops about poverty.

It is all very reasonable, even attractive. It is hard to call any of these
tendencies wrong. And yet I find this sensibility to be an obstacle to an
effective social policy. That is because, in its very reasonableness, the
Catholic mind rarely holds anyone *clearly* responsible for anything. No
clear mandate rests on the individual or on government. Each element in
the system is allowed to look to the others. The poor can expect salvation
to come from the various authorities that are arrayed above them, as in the
medieval great chain of being. These authorities, in turn, can assume that

those who deal with poverty below them are shouldering the major burdens. The Catholic policy analyst concludes, in Mary Jo's words,

> [T]hat all people have responsibilities to their communities; that communities have responsibilities to ensure opportunities for human flourishing to all their members, . . . and that government can be an appropriate means for exercising such care, providing that the rights and responsibilities of lower levels of social organization are respected and met.

Such a formulation does not give clear marching orders to anyone. "For if the trumpet give an uncertain sound, who shall prepare himself to the battle?"[14]

Especially, the Catholic sensibility allows everyone in the system to concentrate on the feel-good side of social policy, which is extending aid to the needy. Everyone can assume that someone else will take on the harder task, which is to get those aided to help themselves. In their political role, this is mostly what the Catholic Church and other denominations have done. In Washington, church bodies call on government in a prophetic voice to be generous to the poor, while assuming that church schools and other local agencies will carry out the moral instruction of the poor. In the end, government has had to assume the enforcing role, in welfare, in law enforcement, and in setting standards in the schools. The churches then are free to criticize that effort for its insensitivity. They can keep their hands clean, while policymakers have to govern.

I, and I believe most Americans, prefer a more clear-cut system in which the benefits of social programs and any obligations linked to them came essentially from the national level. The implications for the common citizenship are too important for the system to vary in any fundamental way around the country. The duty of localities is to implement that system. The duty of recipients is to claim the benefits if they need to and to comply with the system's requirements. This setup is pretty much what we have at present.

In AFDC/TANF, admittedly, benefit levels vary widely, because states have controlled them ever since the creation of AFDC in 1935. But much the same kinds of people were covered in every state. PRWORA devolves many further details of welfare policy to states and local government, appearing to dissolve any national policy. But the localities have used their new authority is remarkably consistent ways across the country. There has been little change in the level of benefits or in who gets them. No state to my knowledge has cut benefits sharply or curbed coverage for mothers under the age of eighteen or for children born on the rolls, as TANF allows them to do. And TANF imposes activity norms for work programs that are uniform across the country. Most states also have chosen similar work goals, aimed at moving recipients quickly into jobs. These new work standards are much the greatest change TANF has made.

Policy

Mary Jo and I disagree surprisingly little about policy. The reason may be that here is where empirical evidence has greatest authority, a point I enlarge on below. We both know what research has to say about which programs have accomplished the most for the working-age poor and their children.

From Catholic social teaching, one might expect a benefit-oriented response—recommendations mainly for new benefits and services for the poor. This is fitting for groups, such as the aged and the disabled, who face no work expectation. For the employable poor, Mary Jo endorses education and training programs to enhance skills, but she makes no large claims for them. The reason is simply that the evaluations of such programs have been less positive than those of the mandatory work programs tied to AFDC/TANF. She also suggests job creation programs, if carefully targeted and implemented. I see little harm in this, but again the record of such programs is not encouraging.

Among income programs, she endorses the earned income tax credit, a federal subsidy for low-paid workers, as I also do. This program, which was sharply expanded in 1993, enjoys broad support precisely because it makes aid contingent on work. Further increases could be considered as a way of raising the low incomes of many mothers who have left welfare for work. The drawback is the same as with any work incentive: the initial benefits give low-wage workers more reason to work, but as their incomes rise, they also lose these benefits, and this can make moving up to a better job seem less worthwhile.

Mary Jo also endorses food stamps, coupons redeemable for groceries that are available to the poor of virtually all descriptions. The food stamp program is the nearest thing we have to a universal income guarantee; it is less controversial than cash welfare because the benefits are more difficult to abuse. The program supports many more working poor than AFDC/TANF did before reform. On the other hand, many of the adult recipients appear to work far less consistently than they could. The food stamp program does have its own work requirements, but they are less stringent and less well implemented than those of TANF. I am torn between the desire to use this program, like cash aid, as a lever to raise work levels and the desire to keep an ultimate income guarantee available.

The strongest controversies still cluster around TANF, notwithstanding the dramatic changes already wrought by PRWORA. I share some of Mary Jo's concern that the reformed aid system will promote overly discretionary administration. Any obligations tied to welfare should apply broadly, not to narrow groups, and should be enforced in a legally defensible way by public officials acting openly with the mandate of the people. In the application of norms to individual cases, however, some discretion is unavoidable.

PRWORA also delegated much more control of welfare to the states, and they in turn have delegated it further to local governments and to many nonprofit and even proprietary agencies. I share Mary Jo's concern about how workable this structure is. In some states, the efforts to reorganize welfare administration have led to confusion. Fortunately, the experience of the last five years is reassuring, in regard to both discretion and devolution. Administrative abuses and problems have occurred but not on a scale that would put reform in question. Most localities appear to have executed the law at least with good intentions and usually with good results.[15]

I agree with Mary Jo that fears of encouraging single-parent families should not deter government from offering aid to families; the evidence that welfare actually causes unwed pregnancy is too weak. Nor should some conservatives' desire to promote marriage through welfare reform be given much scope as yet. That effort still lacks broad public support, and programs that clearly can promote marriage and prevent unwed childbearing have not yet appeared. I would encourage conservatives who favor these programs to develop them further, and then sell them to the public. If and when they succeed, then this agenda should move forward. The reauthorization of TANF may well contain some new funding for these purposes.

Most surprisingly, Mary Jo accepts work requirements in TANF. She finds it fair to expect welfare mothers to work when most other mothers already are doing so. Just as important, recipients told her that they valued the "push" that the requirements gave them to act on their own intentions to work. It is the same argument for paternalism that I make. Mary Jo also respects the clear evidence of the last decade that work requirements, if coupled with new benefits and a bountiful economy, really can raise work levels and incomes and help solve the welfare problem. On the other hand, she shares some of my caution about raising work requirements too much in the current reauthorization.

Immigration

The issue where we disagree most strongly probably is immigration. This is an important question that may well replace welfare as the leading controversy in social policy. There is a connection to welfare, because PRWORA sharply restricted the eligibility of legal aliens for several means-tested benefits. But the subject would be important on its own.

Immigration is the main reason why Hispanics are a rapidly growing component of our population. In 2001, for the first time, they outnumbered blacks, becoming the largest minority.[16] Mary Jo recognizes that Hispanics lack the same historic claims to redress enjoyed by blacks. Most of them come to this country voluntarily, to seek a better life, not as slaves. Most also have not faced the degree of discrimination suffered by blacks. But despite this, she favors an accepting policy toward them. This appears to be mandated by Scripture. The Old Testament tells Jews to welcome the alien and the stranger, while immigrants would appear to be the sort of outsider whom Jesus befriends. She also finds it "hard to justify raising barriers to entry or excluding some people from the resources of the society."

My view is more cautious, on both theological and policy grounds. I doubt that the country has an obligation to welcome all those who might wish to immigrate here. Given worsening conditions in the third world, that might mean hundreds of millions of people. Immigration of that scale would transform the United States beyond recognition, most would say for the worse. Are we obligated to do this simply because these people now have less than we do? I prefer a reading of the gospels in which our moral obligation to others is primarily to those close to us, with whom we already have some relationship. That means our own families, friends, and connections, then the poor of our own locality, then other poor who already are part of this society.[17]

This is an area where policymakers must adopt a civic approach, placing good consequences above attractive intentions. I think the current level and manner of immigration is imprudent. More by drift than decision, the United States has opened itself to a flow of immigrants that could well damage the society, notwithstanding the great benefits the country has drawn from immigration in the past. One problem is that new immigrants to the country are predominantly low-skilled; a higher proportion of skilled immigrants would be worth more to the economy. Another problem is that the predominance of Hispanic immigrants in some localities is threatening the power of the English language, and schooling in English, to integrate the newcomers.

Immigration at current levels might well exacerbate poverty. Immigrants tend to drive down wages for low-skill workers, making it tougher for our current poor, especially blacks, to escape need. And immigrants' descendants may swell the underclass. We usually think of immigrants as only temporarily poor. Classically, they enter this country penniless, but then they learn English, become educated in our public schools, work hard, enter the middle class, and enjoy the American dream. That still happens, but disquieting evidence exists that the children of some recent black and Hispanic immigrants, when they encounter racism, identify downward with the current poor and adopt an "oppositional" stance toward society.[18]

There could also be adverse effects on the political culture. Good government is crucial to the success of welfare reform and other complex antipoverty measures.[19] Immigration tends inherently to reduce government quality, simply because immigrants tend to come from troubled societies less civic than our own. In the nineteenth century, rapid immigration chiefly from Europe was one cause of widespread political corruption in

American cities, a problem that political reform took decades to overcome. Similar damage seems to be occurring now in the cities and regions of the country most exposed to immigration. Illegal immigration undermines legality across the country. Businesses that hire illegals—and even families seeking household help—find themselves operating outside the law.

Immigration certainly should continue; it fuels the development of our economy and our culture. But the level should be reduced to what the nation can absorb without threatening its cohesion or its institutions. The greatest problem is illegal immigration; it somehow must be converted to legal. In part, that requires keeping undocumented aliens out by controlling the borders and deterring their employment by placing stronger sanctions on businesses that hire them. The economy does need labor, but amnesty for illegal immigrants, such as the Bush administration has discussed, would undermine the rule of law yet further and swell the illegal inflow. A compromise might be to send some illegals home, then readmit them legally, provided they had been steadily employed and not broken laws or abused programs while in this country.

The above discussion may sound too hard-headed. Mary Jo uses more earnest, theological language. Realism may seem to block doing good. But the Bible tells us to be "wise as serpents" as well as "innocent as doves."[20] Historically, the United States has been a force that advances values that have religious origins—freedom, democracy, human rights. But to continue to do that, it cannot become just another country, which is what ungoverned immigration eventually would make it. It must remain "a light unto the nations," and for this, preserving its civic qualities is essential.[21] I place that priority ahead of welcoming all those who want to come to these shores.

Norms and Facts

An important convention of Catholic social teaching is that theology is more important than the details. As Mary Jo says, commentators may differ in their application of the tradition to current problems, but "to a large extent, the disagreements turn on facts and predictions and on differences in emphasis rather than on theology."

To a great extent that is true, and not only among Catholics. The values that the popes and bishops honor in their social teaching, such as the "dignity" of the individual and the importance of compassion, are shared as well by the larger political order. That is hardly surprising. The Christian tradition, much of it Catholic, is the crucible that formed the moral values of modern politics. Western governments see individuals as important and seek their happiness and development because they were taught to do so by churches over centuries.

It also is a feature of our current politics that moral values and principles are less in question than they were fifty years ago.[22] Before the 1960s, American politics was dominated by the traditional partisan struggle over whether to have more government or less. In this era, which I call progressive, the master issue was whether the terms of belonging and reward in society should be set by the marketplace or by government. Should there be capitalism or collectivism? In this politics, the values of the society were profoundly at issue. There still is a partisan division on these questions, as every controversy over the budget or tax cuts shows. But in practice, the possible change in the scope of government is small compared with what it used to be.

The emergence of the poverty problem in the 1960s led to a very different politics. Whereas the struggle of the working class for economic gains and of blacks for civil rights had raised issues of justice, poverty tended rather to raise issues of order. Questions of social reform were shoved off the agenda, and instead politicians debated how to restore civility within society. The key dispute now was how far one could hold the poor, rather than society, responsible for good behavior. Behind that issue lay the question of how competent the poor were to manage their own lives. These judgments about responsibility and competence had to do with human nature rather than the more impersonal structures of society.

Whereas progressive politics inspired a clash of ideologies, poverty politics tends to be moralistic and empirical. Everyone accepts that government ought to promote equal opportunity, but people disagree on whether that goal is realized in practice. Is there still discrimination against minorities and women? Can the poor really find the jobs and child care they need to avoid welfare? These issues are fought over by social scientists and by lawyers prosecuting discrimination cases in the courts. But behind the factual disputes, different views about human nature divide those who see barriers from those who do not. Another strongly empirical issue is what sort of antipoverty program works best. The public interventions of the progressive era, such as union rights or the Social Security program, could be justified in simple moral terms without the need for evaluation. Antipoverty programs, however, are viewed more as means to ends. They must be justified by results.

As Mary Jo notes, some of the disagreements over Catholic social teaching are ideological. But others come down to these concrete issues of program effectiveness. The strong authority of the facts explains why her policy recommendations converge with mine, even though our theological rationales differ. Indeed, I find that her recommendations put pressure on her rationale. Her endorsement of work requirements jibes in a general way with statements by the popes and bishops about mutual responsibility—but it does contradict their injunctions against making mothers work. To this extent, facts finally take priority over values.[23]

As some have noted, there is a similar tension between the way local Catholic caregivers relate to the poor and the measures that Catholic leaders advocate in Washington. Catholic parochial schools are famous among policy analysts for their success at educating poor children, black and white, Catholic and non-Catholic alike. These schools appear to succeed largely because they are paternalistic. They combine genuine care for their students with an insistence on order and standards. The public schools in ghetto areas seldom do as well.[24] Other Catholic agencies—those caring for runaway youth or the homeless, for example—are similarly structured, enforcing the rules on those they serve. Yet at a political level, church leaders typically oppose policies placing any demands on the poor, which they see as threatening social commitment to the needy. Local caregivers, however, see what actually helping the poor requires. Again, experience—evidence—trumps theological reasoning.

The chief place where values differ in social politics today is in matters related to the family—especially divorce and abortion. These issues are contentious in part because they are neglected in secular political thinking. No traditional ideology—whether liberalism, conservatism, or communism—had much to say about the family. All focused on individuals or on workers, on the public world rather than the private, and on men more than women. Take care of (largely male) workers, it was assumed, and you would also take care of families, including spouses and children. Today Catholics and the religious right want to restrict or forbid divorce and abortion, while committed secularists believe that people must be left free to choose whether to continue their relationships or their pregnancies. The issues are tough to compromise precisely because they concern principles rather than judgments about facts or programs.

But in a sense religion also is to blame. The Bible evades family issues almost as much as secular ideologies do. Most of its ethical teaching is about how people should relate to each other outside the family or to God. It says remarkably little about how to handle the conflicts that arise in one's personal life. Perhaps these differences are simply too painful and tragic to deal with more fully. Catholics see Jesus' few statements on marriage as barring divorce; believing that life arises at conception, they also oppose abortion as a form of murder. Other creeds regret divorce and abortion without explicitly forbidding them.

The reticence of the texts, plus the difficulty of the subjects, helps to explain why we have not worked out a modus vivendi in these subjects as we have on other questions in social policy. In other areas, we manage to combine forgiveness and standards, just as Jesus does. We are learning how to help the needy while still expecting a measure of work and other civilities from them. Through public programs, we help those who lose a job to get another, but employment remains demanding. Through lenient bankruptcy laws, we tell people who fail in business to try again, but launching a business is still difficult. Few think that by this assistance we undermine social standards. But we have not learned how to free people from impossible situations in their private lives while still defending the sanctity of marriage and the family. We seem to face a choice between forgiveness *or* standards, the very thing that Jesus avoids.

Notes

1. See particularly Mary Jo Bane and David T. Ellwood, "Slipping into and out of Poverty: The Dynamics of Spells," *Journal of Human Resources*, vol. 21, no. 1 (Winter 1986), pp. 1–23; and Mary Jo Bane and David T. Ellwood, *Welfare Realities: From Rhetoric to Reform* (Harvard University Press, 1994).

2. Lawrence M. Mead, *The New Politics of Poverty: The Nonworking Poor in America* (New York: Basic Books, 1992), chapters 4–9.

3. B. J. Malina, "Wealth and Poverty in the New Testament and Its World," *Interpretation*, vol. 41, no. 4 (October 1987), pp. 354–66; Allen Verhey, *Remembering Jesus: Christian Community, Scripture, and the Moral Life* (Grand Rapids, Mich.: Eerdmans, 2002), chapter 13.

4. John R. Schneider, *The Good of Affluence: Seeking God in a Culture of Wealth* (Grand Rapids, Mich.: Eerdmans, 2002), chapter 1.

5. This is my difference with Douglas S. Massey and Nancy A. Denton, *American Apartheid: Segregation and the Making of the Underclass* (Harvard University Press, 1993).

6. U.S. Bureau of the Census, *Statistical Abstract of the United States 2002* (U.S. Government Printing Office, December 2002), pp. 59, 202.

7. James Q. Wilson, "Slavery and the Black Family," *Public Interest*, vol. 147 (Spring 2002), pp. 3–23.

8. Joseph H. Carens, "Rights and Duties in an Egalitarian Society," *Political Theory*, vol. 14, no. 1 (February 1986), pp. 31–49.

9. Mark 10:17–22.

10. George Lakoff, *Moral Politics: What Conservatives Know That Liberals Don't* (University of Chicago Press, 1996).

11. Psalm 19:10.

12. Matthew 25:14–30; Luke 19:11–26.

13. Schneider, *Good of Affluence*, p. 192.

14. I Corinthians 14:8. This quotation is from the King James version.

15. I base this assessment on case studies of TANF implementation done by the Urban Institute and the Rockefeller Institute of Government at the State University of New York.

16. U.S. Bureau of the Census, *Poverty in the United States: 2001*, Current Population Reports, P60-219 (U.S. Government Printing Office, September 2002), table A-1. Technically, Hispanics are not a racial but an ethnic category. They may be of any race. Enough of them are nonwhite, however, for the group to be treated in political and policy terms as racial.

17. Schneider, *Good of Affluence*, pp. 87–9, 172–82, calls this the principle of "moral proximity."

18. Christopher Jencks, "Who Should Get In?" *New York Review of Books*, November 29, 2001, pp. 57–63; Jencks, "Who Should Get In? Part II," *New York Review of Books*, December 20, 2001, pp. 94–102.

19. Lawrence M. Mead, "Welfare Reform: The Institutional Dimension," *Focus*, vol. 22, no. 1 (special issue 2002): 39–46. I set out this argument more fully in Mead, *Government Matters: Welfare Reform in Wisconsin* (Princeton University Press, 2004).

20. Matthew 10:16.

21. Isaiah 42:6.

22. The following draws on Mead, *New Politics of Poverty*, chapters 1–3, 10–11.

23. For a similar analysis of poverty from a more conservative Catholic perspective, see Michael Novak and others, *The New Consensus on Family and Welfare: A Community of Self-Reliance* (Washington: American Enterprise Institute, 1987). This was the report of the Working Seminar on Family and American Welfare Policy, a bipartisan group of experts that influenced the Family Support Act of 1988. Drafted by Michael Novak, a Catholic theologian, it also embraces work requirements.

24. James S. Coleman, Thomas Hoffer, and Sally Kilgore, *High School Achievement: Public, Catholic and Private Schools Compared* (New York: Basic Books, 1982).

PERSONAL RESPONSIBILITY MEANS
SOCIAL RESPONSIBILITY

MARY JO BANE

Larry observes that our dialogue thus far reveals that he and I differ rather little in our poverty and welfare policy prescriptions, that we differ more in our definitions and explanations of the poverty problem, and that we differ most in our theological interpretations. This observation raises interesting implications and questions, some of them disquieting. One possibility is that one or the other of us is not moving logically from theology to policy. For example, Larry implies that my policy prescriptions, with which he mostly agrees, are inconsistent with my theology, with which he does not agree—presumably suggesting that I should revise my theology. This is a troubling notion. Alternatively, one could infer that if two people who disagree on theology can agree on policy, then theology must not matter much. This too would be a disconcerting conclusion.

In this response, I will deal mainly with the extent to which Larry's observation is accurate, with possible explanations of our agreements and disagreements, and with the implications for the interaction of policy and theology more generally.

Policy

Despite the fact that Larry and I have on more than one occasion testified on different sides of a policy or legislative issue, our disagreements on concrete current poverty and welfare policies are relatively minor—increasingly so, as we have clarified our positions over the course of this

140

dialogue. Larry suggests that our general agreement on concrete policy issues comes from the fact that we are both social scientists, immersed in the empirical literature, an observation with which I agree. We both also are what might be called radical incrementalists. We have been involved enough in both politics and the ground-level workings of programs to have a pretty good sense of what is and is not possible. We read public opinion polls and legislative debates as well as the social science literature. And neither of us spends our time analyzing or advocating policies, however theoretically attractive, that could never be passed into law, or if passed, actually implemented.

I suspect, as Larry does, that the empirical and practical orientation of our policy analyses explains our agreements. I find that reassuring and hope that our readers find it reassuring as well. It suggests that men and women can come together and solve narrowly defined but important problems, in this and in other policy arenas, on the basis of evidence or of reasonable compromises on how to proceed in the absence of definitive evidence—and do so within a broadly shared framework of principles and values, despite real or apparent disagreements on some of the important background issues.

At the same time, differences on definitions, explanations, principles, and theological underpinnings are important in thinking beyond incrementalism, for shaping a moral stance, for establishing priorities, and for dealing with uncertainty. Larry and I differ, for example, on how broadly we define the problem of poverty and on the extent to which policy needs to address structural and institutional barriers rather than focus on dysfunctional behavior. The roots of these differences are worth exploring.

The Problem and Its Explanations

Larry and I agree that there exists a group of Americans that seem to be stuck in long-term poverty accompanied by isolation from the mainstream economy and polity. Whether one sees this group as one among many important groups among the poor, as I do, or as the only group requiring serious policy reflection, as Larry does, its existence cries out for explanation—on which Larry and I differ. Larry describes me as holding a "moderate version" of "sociologism," which he defines as "the attribution of poverty and dependency to barriers of opportunity outside the poor themselves." He challenges this view on empirical and biblical grounds and also argues that it leads to bad policy, specifically policy that is ineffective in addressing dependency and social isolation.

An interesting aspect of Larry's argument is his suggestion that "social barriers have much more to do . . . with the highly unequal incomes found among working Americans. . . . barriers explain inequality better than they do poverty." Later, he says "in explaining *poverty*, race counts for less than in explaining overall racial inequality." This distinction reflects Larry's view that poverty is largely a problem of nonwork, which he explains as a problem of dysfunctional behavior. Although he is willing to attribute inequality among workers to structural and racial barriers, he sees such barriers as much less important in explaining poverty, that is, nonwork.

Larry's position conceptualizes poverty, then, as being qualitatively different from the state of the rest of the population, rather than as describing the condition of those at the bottom of the distribution of income or participation. The conventional notions of poverty recognize that defining it requires drawing a more or less arbitrary line through a distribution. Where the poverty line is drawn in rich countries is inherently relative: the poor are those who are some distance away from the mainstream, often measured by median income. The conventionally drawn poverty line in the United States counts among the poor badly educated workers stuck in low-paying jobs; families that have temporarily fallen on hard times because of layoffs, natural disasters, or other misfortunes; and elderly people if their household income falls below the line. Larry admits that structural and institutional barriers are causal in these cases, but he does not consider these cases very important in discussions of poverty policy. I do.

Larry also asserts that the barriers erected by racial discrimination or by institutional shortcomings in the labor market or in the education, health, or social service systems matter little in explaining the plight of the contemporary long-term nonworking poor. I simply disagree. I do not claim that behaviors—choices about schooling, family formation, work, criminal activity, and so on—are not implicated; such a claim would not only ignore empirical reality but also deny the ability of the poor to shape their

142

own destinies. I do claim that behaviors and barriers interact and that we need to attend to such issues as the continuing legacy of racial stigma, the continuing failure of many urban school systems, and the lack of fit between the current labor market and the situations of many potential workers. Larry argues that these barriers have been largely removed, at least as causes of poverty. I contend, on the other hand, that it remains unreasonable to expect that without continuing attention to the remaining barriers people will be able to improve their lot significantly through the sheer force of will alone. I therefore argue that an antipoverty agenda must speak to these structural and institutional issues.

It is important to note that in explaining long-term poverty, both Larry and I say *both*; *both* individual and institutional characteristics, *both* culture and structure. But we put different emphasis on one or the other sort of explanation in suggesting an overall policy agenda. And we tend to err on different sides when it comes to situations of uncertainty. These differences are real, and they relate to the framework, including the religious interpretation, that we bring to policy debate.

Theology

Both of us also say *both* in reading Scripture. Larry is quite right to challenge a portrait of the Jesus of the gospels that paints him as one-dimensional or wishy-washy, as favoring only the poor, or as demanding of only a few rich. Jesus placed stunning demands on his disciples: to leave their parents, to sell all their possessions and give the proceeds to the poor, to "drink of the cup" of suffering and death that Jesus himself would experience.[1] And although Jesus clearly called twelve of his disciples in a special way, he called, and calls, all men and women to follow him. We ignore Jesus' demands, on ourselves and on others, at our peril. A challenge of the gospel and a mystery of our faith is to know and to live in the knowledge that all of us are both unconditionally loved and accepted by God and also fully claimed by God and called to a life of complete and radical obedience to God's plan. Christian discipleship is not for the faint of heart. But neither is it for an elite who then relate to the rest of humanity with condescension, however compassionate, nor for a different kind of elite who see the need for sacrifice only in others.

Theological writing, no doubt including my own amateur efforts, often fails to convey the full, rich, radical gospel message. Historically, the Christian church was all too comfortable with a social structure that was hierarchical and in the extreme feudal. Clergy and church leaders often identified with the elite to the extent that they preached to the poor the virtues of passivity and deference, with the promise of eternal reward in the next world for submitting to their betters in this one. Much of contemporary theology challenges that history. The articulation of a gospel-mandated preference for the poor rightly confronts the indifference to or oppression of the poor by the allegedly Christian rich, especially in developing countries. Liberation theology challenges the historical and institutional tendency of the church in some countries to identify with the rich and to consciously or unconsciously become complicit in the exploitation of the poor. But these concepts, applied indiscriminately, can lead to romanticizing or patronizing the poor, thereby excluding them from full membership in the community, which expects personal responsibility and repentance as well as self-giving and radical generosity—from all, toward all.

Larry is right to identify this excluding tendency as fundamentally unbiblical. Jesus' preference for the poor is a preference for fully including in his community the outcasts of the larger society. I hope Larry is wrong in seeing condescension in my own theology. I believe he is wrong in seeing it behind the long-running opposition of the Catholic hierarchy to work requirements for mothers, which I believe derives from another source. This issue is worth spending a few sentences on, since it seems to be the main basis for Larry's belief that my policy positions are incompatible with my theology, which he correctly interprets as generally consistent with Catholic social teachings.

The Catholic hierarchy has indeed opposed work requirements for AFDC/TANF recipients, most of whom, of course, are mothers. Their opposition can be read, however, as pertaining more to motherhood than to work. The Catholic hierarchy struggles, unsuccessfully in the view of many, with issues related to the roles and status of women. The hierarchy continues to see women's main vocation as motherhood and to advocate a gender-based division of labor in the home. In this view, ideally mothers should not have to work or aspire to work; nor should mothers be required to work by either economic circumstances or the requirements of welfare programs. The Catholic bishops, in their generally progressive policy approach to poverty in their letter on the economy, said: "We affirm the principle that society's institutions and policies should be structured so that mothers of young children are not forced by economic necessity to leave their children for jobs outside the home."[2] Larry should not be surprised to learn that I disagree with the views of the hierarchy of my church on women.[3] My own position on work requirements recognizes that women of all marital and economic statuses now work, that their working is appropriate, and that fairness suggests that if mothers not on welfare must work, then mothers on welfare also ought to work. Fairness also requires, I believe, that both workplace and welfare regimes be responsive to the responsibilities of parents of both genders. Thus, like Larry, I oppose unreasonable demands in terms of hours of work in both settings. These views, I believe, are quite consistent with the broad social justice tradition of the church.

That aside, however, it is not at all obvious that because the gospel is demanding, Christians should support work requirements in government programs any more than they should support a universal negative income tax because the gospel is compassionate. The analogies are by no means straightforward. Jesus' demands were not about work; in fact, he expected his disciples to leave their nets in the boat, to leave the field unplowed and even the parent unburied. He called for indifference to bodily needs—observe the flowers of the field—and extreme generosity: if someone asks for your tunic, give him your cloak as well. Jesus did not instruct his disciples to preach a gospel of requirements; they were to preach both repentance and forgiveness.[4] And as Larry quite correctly points out, Jesus had nothing to say about legislation or policy formation in democratic societies.

This raises the extremely important and difficult question of whether and how one moves or tries to move from theology to policy. For many Christians, the move from gospel to personal morality is one of analogy, an attempt to discern what it would mean to imitate Christ in a specific personal situation. But analogies work less well for thinking about policy in a pluralist democratic society with a constitution based not on "What would Jesus do?" but on mutually accepted obligations of justice. The

Catholic theological tradition articulates principles of social justice applicable in a secular society by relying on diverse sources of authority and modes of argument. For Catholics, Scripture is not the only source of authority; tradition, reason, and experience also are important. In their 1986 pastoral letter on the economy, for example, the Catholic bishops begin with Scripture to ground their basic commitment to the dignity of all men and women, to the importance of community, and to the obligations of justice. They then articulate a set of ethical principles, which they frame in secular language and argue as generally applicable on the basis of reason and experience, to which all have access.[5] I attempted something similar in my opening essay by exploring the principles of a preference for the poor, mutual responsibility, and subsidiarity through both scriptural interpretation and secular argument.

It is interesting that the middle-level principles of justice that the bishops and I articulated have much in common with Larry's three principles of sustenance, community, and autonomy. The ethical argument of the bishops, built on a long tradition of discernment and analysis, provides a basis for their and for my emphasis on the first two of these principles, sometimes at the cost of the third. The point here, though, is that the gospel is not the only source of the argument and that it is not necessary to use the language of the gospel in articulating the argument. Good theological ethics, like good policy analysis, brings together foundational narratives (Scripture, the Constitution), ethical principles (distributive justice, mutual obligations), history, and experience. The bishops provide a model of this in their letter on the economy.

That letter also illustrates the need for continuing dialogue and for attention to empirical and practical realities. Their 1986 policy prescriptions—which even at the time they advanced tentatively—now seem quite disconnected from contemporary political and social reality. That is illustrated not only by their opposition to work requirements but also by their arguments for more centralization and federal direction of welfare programs. I have tried to bring their methods and their principles into a more sophisticated and contemporary understanding of policy. I have also tried to make explicit what I have called a Catholic sensibility, a set of orientations toward the world that come into play in situations of uncertainty, in which neither facts nor reasoned argument about principles can definitively determine a policy recommendation.

For me, both the foundation and methodology of Catholic social teaching and the Catholic sensibility are relevant to policy. Larry challenges the relevance of theology, a question to which I now turn.

A Catholic Policy Analyst?

I propose here to explore the question of relevance from two perspectives, that of a policy analyst or public official who happens to be Catholic and that of the parties who represent in policy discussions the teaching office of the Catholic church, specifically, the staff of the National Conference of Catholic Bishops and of Catholic Charities USA. In both cases I speak from my own experience but with attention to broader questions.

Over the years, I have written much about poverty and welfare policy and taken positions on many issues, both general and specific. I have written both as an academic and as an appointed public official. This dialogue represents the first occasion, outside of explicitly liturgical settings, on which I have grounded my argument in the language of Catholic social teachings. Since the argument here is not fundamentally different from arguments I have made in the past, it may be worth asking what, if anything, the religious language adds and why I have not employed it in the past, aside from the fact that no one else was doing so.

The answer is not a simple distinction between public and private life. My Christian identity influences my private moral life, of course, but it also underlies my specific research and teaching interests, and it brought me into public service in the first place. It inevitably shapes the assumptions that I make about human beings and the ethical principles that lie behind my policy analyses. But those basic assumptions and ethical commitments are widely shared in the contemporary United States, and they can be articulated in a shared secular language as well as religious language. We can talk about humanity as created in the image of God or as inherently equal; we can talk about the beloved community or about responsibilities rooted in a social contract; we can advocate subsidiarity or federalism. I am not, I believe, being dishonest in using nonreligious language in public discussion, nor do I believe that by doing so I am either ignoring my Catholic beliefs or sneaking them into the public sphere.

But it is interesting to ask whether the kind of dialogue that Larry and I have had in these pages might enrich public discussion if more of us used both religious and secular language in our deliberations. As long as we open our positions, whether based on religious or secular beliefs, for examination, argument, and potential modification, we are proceeding in a way consistent with the democratic process in our pluralist society. It may well be that including explicitly religious voices can aid rather than detract from society's search for an overlapping consensus on the values that undergird policy.[6]

Articulating and clarifying values certainly is an appropriate role for academic policy analysts and public officials. Public and political positions often turn on values. For example, the public's anger at the pre-1996 welfare system came at least in part from perceptions of unfairness in the system: that some people worked and took responsibility for their children while others did not have to. But public opinion polls also revealed a strong commitment to helping the poor, especially poor children.[7] Articulating and examining the underlying values, tracing their implications, and identifying situations in which important values may be in tension with each other can be extremely useful for those who speak and write about poverty. Perhaps doing so can be made even more useful by expanding the modes of discourse that we use, since the ethical values of so many among the American public are rooted in their religious commitments. Currently, the articulation of religious values in public life is carried out for the most part by religious professionals in national denominational offices, a group to which I now turn.

Catholic Policy Advocacy?

Throughout, Larry expresses displeasure with what he calls the institutional church, usually referring to statements of either the Catholic bishops or the offices of the mainline Protestant denominations. Larry chides them for being irrelevant and out of touch with both American society and their own authentic theology. I have a somewhat different quarrel with the advocacy efforts of the national Catholic bodies. Both sets of criticisms suggest the possibility of a different, more appropriate, and therefore more relevant stance for religious professionals.

During the debates over the 1996 welfare reform bill, which I observed from within the Clinton administration, the National Council of Catholic Bishops and Catholic Charities USA developed both general positions on the legislation and stands on specific provisions. These positions derived both from Catholic social teachings and from the institutional interests of the Catholic Church. For example, the Catholic groups supported retention of the entitlement nature of AFDC, opposed work requirements for mothers of very young children, opposed the family cap (which they feared could lead to increases in abortion), and supported increased funding for child welfare services (an important funding source for Catholic Charities agencies).[8] In general, their positions were somewhat to the left of that of the administration and close to the positions of the more liberal members of the House.

Professionals from both groups testified in public hearings and also interacted with individual members of Congress. My sense was that they were very good at what they did: they were well informed, armed with evidence, sensitive to the concerns of individual members of Congress, articulate, and willing to cooperate in forging compromises. They seemed to be listened to by congressional staff and respected for their professionalism and moral commitments. As best I could tell, however, their level of effectiveness was not much different from that of the also very competent government affairs staffs of other progressive advocacy groups. They were not treated as though they represented 45 million (the approximate number of adult Catholics) potential voters. They were respected but not feared.

And, of course, they did not represent 45 million potential voters. Catholic public opinion was barely more liberal on welfare than American public opinion in general. Many, perhaps the majority, among Catholics opposed the positions on entitlement, work, family caps, and government spending that the official groups were advocating. At the time my reaction to this was to regret the relative ineffectiveness of the Catholic lobbyists; I thought they were on the right side of the issues and wanted them to have a more powerful voice. I wanted them to turn out a

grassroots base—marches, phone calls, letters to members of Congress—
of the sort they periodically turn out on abortion-related issues.

But observing how the Catholic lobbyists actually operated raised
interesting questions about their role and particularly about their relationship to ordinary Catholics in parishes. In general, there was little
interaction. Policy positions were not developed in collaboration with
parish Catholics, nor were they forcefully articulated by preachers at Sunday liturgies. I do not want to argue here that the policy positions taken
by the official Catholic bodies should simply reflect the opinions of
Catholics—that they should take a poll and abide by it. Even less do I
want to argue that the hierarchy should take inflexible positions on social
justice issues that they then communicate to the Catholic faithful as
dogma to be deferentially accepted—the strategy that the hierarchy tries
to follow, partly successfully, concerning abortion. Nonetheless, interaction is essential for both good religious practice and good politics.

Catholic ecclesiological structure includes a teaching office that has a
mandate to speak from and for the tradition on important moral issues;
that mandate and the mission of the teaching office also permit it to speak
and even lobby on contemporary policy issues that involve moral judgment. The office can and does, however, act inappropriately in three ways.
First, it sometimes equates its authority to speak on moral issues with the
authority to speak on empirical issues. Larry criticizes the hierarchy for
taking positions that fail to reflect social science evaluations of their efficiency or effectiveness; I would put the hierarchy's sometimes naïve advocacy of job creation programs in this category. Second, it often fails to
understand that moral discernment is a responsibility of the entire people
of God, not just of a small group of religious professionals in Washington
offices. This amounts to equating the hierarchy with the church, a mistake
clearly identified by Vatican Council II and by the theologians who have
articulated a post–Vatican II ecclesiology.[9] Third, making an analogous
theological (and political) error, it often seems to assume that a small
group of Washington professionals can speak legitimately and effectively
for the people of God without their active participation and consent.

I believe that the proper role for the national religious bodies in the
contemporary U.S. context is both to shape and to articulate the moral

sense of the church community, to engage the community in a process of deliberating policy that brings in both moral and empirical considerations, and to communicate the outcome of that deliberation in the national arena.

Sometimes the shaping role must be prominent and prophetic. The church as an institution needed to speak strongly against slavery and against genocide (which in several instances it nevertheless did not do). It feels called to speak uncompromisingly against abortion, which it sees as an evil equivalent to slavery. John Paul II, to his great credit, regularly speaks in a strong prophetic voice about the obligations of rich countries to developing countries.

In ordinary times or on more ordinary issues, the institutional church could better serve its mission, both internally and externally, by becoming more respectful of democracy, both internal and external. The institutional structures of the church could generate in parishes the kind of deliberation that Larry and I have carried on in these pages. It would start with the Scriptures and the various legitimate readings of the Scriptures. It would pose issues, look at facts, clarify value conflicts, and identify areas of crucial disagreement around facts and predictions. It would help people problem solve—or, alternatively, help them to articulate different but principled and supported positions. It would bring elected officials or aspiring elected officials to listen to these deliberations and to judge what the people of God are saying and what values they may bring into the voting booth.

There is, of course, the danger that if ordinary Catholics are encouraged by their hierarchy to deliberate on issues of poverty and welfare, they might also decide to deliberate on sexuality and the infallibility of the pope. No doubt this is why my proposal is unlikely to generate an enthusiastic response in hierarchical circles. But if these issues are ignored, Larry's observation that those who speak for religion are largely irrelevant in public debate is likely to remain true. And that would be a shame.

Notes

1. See, for example, Matthew 10:35–45, 16:24–28, 19:16–30, 20:20–28; Mark 8:34–9:1, 10:17–31, 35–45; and Luke 9:23–27, 18:18–30, 22:24–27.

2. National Conference of Catholic Bishops, *Economic Justice for All: Pastoral Letter on Catholic Social Teaching and the U.S. Economy* (Washington: 1986), p. 207.

3. It is important to note that I articulate this as a disagreement with the hierarchy, not with the church. The views of the hierarchy deserve respect from the faithful, but they are only one aspect of the life of the people of God.

4. See, for example, Matthew 8:19–22, 10:1–6, 12:22–34; Luke 9:59–62.

5. National Conference of Catholic Bishops, *Economic Justice for All*, chapter 2.

6. This argument is well developed in Ronald F. Thiemann, *Religion and Public Life: A Dilemma for Democracy* (Georgetown University Press, 1996).

7. A good discussion of public opinion on welfare is found in R. Kent Weaver, *Ending Welfare as We Know It* (Brookings, 2000), pp. 169–95.

8. Ibid. Weaver describes Catholic Charities as a "service provider" (p. 197) and discusses their activities in his section on child advocacy groups (pp. 199–205).

9. Vatican Council II, "Lumen Gentium: Dogmatic Constitution on the Church," in Austin Flannery and O. P. Northport, eds., *Vatican Council II: The Basic Sixteen Documents* (New York: Costello Publishing, 1995), pp. 1–95. Avery Dulles, a rather conservative theologian (now a cardinal), in *Models of the Church* (Doubleday Image Books, 1987), outlines several models, one of which, the institutional, he rejects for its inability to capture the nature of the church.

GUARANTEE WORK
RATHER THAN AID

LAWRENCE M. MEAD

Mary Jo makes several rejoinders to my essay. Here I respond to her most important points, then offer some broader reflections on why theologians have had little influence on social policy.

Is Work the Problem?

Mary Jo says that I exaggerate the number of poor who are affected by low work levels. She estimates that the nonworking but employable mothers targeted by welfare reform constituted only 2 percent of the poor in 2001. Even if we add up all the adults affected by nonwork, and their dependents, they total only 43 percent of the poor. By my estimate, among poor adults ages eighteen to sixty-four, nonworkers not claiming to be disabled constituted 19 percent of the poor by themselves.[1] If one adds their dependents, plus other poor family heads working less than full time for a full year and their dependents, then Mary Jo's figure is reasonable.

I do not claim that nonworkers are a majority of the poor. Rather, I say that working-age individuals are a majority of the poor and that *whether* they work is strategic for the whole poverty problem. Poor children especially have a large stake in whether their parents work. While the most controversial nonworkers are those on welfare, others are off welfare, including many fathers of welfare families. Thirty-eight percent of poor adults are employed, and they stand a far better chance of escaping poverty than the nonworkers. They include many single mothers who recently left welfare due to reform. Much of our current policy aims at increasing their numbers and supporting them so they can escape poverty through work.

I agree that many and maybe most of the poor are not individually employable at a moment in time; they include children and the elderly and also some of those of working age who face disability or prohibitive personal problems. But most of these unemployable poor probably live in families in which one or more persons are employable and might work more than they do. I also support programs aimed at the unemployable, such as food stamps, Supplemental Security Income (SSI), and Medicaid. None of these programs has been as controversial as AFDC/TANF, and none has been reformed as clearly to enforce work. But it is notable that even people who cannot work often rely on these programs less than they do on earnings from other family members.

When PRWORA transformed AFDC into TANF, it left food stamps and Medicaid little changed, other than restricting the eligibility of aliens. These programs were supposed to remain entitlements, not to be contingent on work as TANF was. The idea was that they would become "work supports" for single-parent families leaving cash welfare for jobs, and for many families they have been. Some mothers work their way off TANF but remain eligible for food stamps and Medicaid, which have higher income eligibility limits. They often also receive child care subsidies and the EITC.

Yet take-up of the noncash benefits nevertheless fell as the TANF rolls came down. Somehow, many mothers who leave cash aid leave the other means-tested programs as well, even when they remain eligible for them. One reason apparently is that food stamps, Medicaid, and child care subsidies used to be administered more or less as a package with AFDC or TANF. Welfare agencies have not always separated out these programs so that families can keep them when they leave cash aid. But another reason appears to be that people leaving cash welfare often want out of the entire welfare system. Even though they may still be eligible for "welfare" in some forms, they are tired of the stigma and the paperwork. They prefer to rely on earnings and employer-based benefits, such as health insurance, to take care of their children and perhaps other relatives. Thus employment ends up supporting many poor people who are not themselves employable.

We also should remember that the employable and unemployable often are the same people at different points in their lives. The national social insurance system created in 1935 presumed that working parents would support their children. If they lost their jobs, they would receive unemployment insurance, to which their employers previously had contributed. If they retired (or, after 1956, became disabled), they could draw Social Security benefits, to which both they and their employers had contributed. Thus either earnings or benefits tied to earnings would support the entire population, even during periods when some people could not work. Welfare in the sense of unearned, means-tested benefits was supposed to decline to a residual role. If it did not, that was chiefly because a substantial population could not fulfill the demands of social insurance due to work and family problems.

By enforcing work in TANF, the government, strongly backed by the public, seeks in essence to adapt welfare to fit the social insurance model. Perhaps welfare benefits have not been earned in advance in the manner of social insurance, but they can be earned while they are received by having adult recipients work alongside the taxpayers. The main point is not to save money or to get labor out of the recipients, although both effects can benefit society. For the most part, it is to exact reciprocity.

Job Programs

Mary Jo is more willing to try out new social programs than I would be, but our difference here is limited. She suggests that job creation programs might be worthwhile when it is doubtful that poor adults who are expected to work can actually find jobs. I accept that if government enforces work as a condition of aid, then in principle it must guarantee jobs. Otherwise, should jobs be unavailable, work tests become just a backhanded way of denying people aid. Everyone prefers that recipients find regular positions, chiefly in the private sector, but if they cannot, then jobs must be created within government.

I say "in principle" because in practice the private sector usually has provided the needed jobs. That fact has allowed mandatory work programs to require recipients to look for work without strictly ensuring it. Rather, recipients search for jobs, and usually within a short period they either find a job or find some other way to leave welfare. Private jobs were particularly plentiful during the implementation of TANF—one reason why the rolls fell so dramatically. But many welfare adults can find work even in less bountiful times, such as the 1980s or even the 1970s. Observers too readily think that high unemployment rates mean that jobs must be unavailable for job seekers. Actually, the economy creates many positions even during a recession, just fewer than during a boom. Viewed at a moment in time, there are fewer openings than there are job seekers. But because openings turn over more rapidly than the jobless, even limited job creation is sufficient to place most unemployed individuals within several weeks or months—provided that they keep looking for work.[2]

Only during the Great Depression, when unemployment hit 25 percent of the labor force, was the government forced to create jobs for the jobless on a large scale. In more recent welfare-work programs, public employment usually has been a small component, used for recipients who appear to be employable but, for whatever reason, fail to find private employment. Under TANF, only New York City and Wisconsin have created jobs on a substantial scale, in both cases because of special conditions. Wisconsin was determined to enforce work in welfare up front, rather than allow people to go on public assistance and then look for work; it could do so fairly only if it provided jobs for the less employable. In New York City, private sector job search programs traditionally had been weak, and work requirements also faced strong resistance from local politicians and community groups. Hence the welfare system's best hope for enforcing work was to do it within the bureaucracy, a setting that government controls.

The main danger I see in further job programs is that they might confuse the chief message of welfare reform, which is that now the responsibility for overcoming poverty is to be shared by poor adults and the government. If government takes continuous new initiatives to help people, that may suggest that it accepts all the responsibility, which was the message of Great Society programs in the 1960s and 1970s.[3] Another danger is that job programs might be administered too leniently, so that job holders are not expected to show up consistently or to work hard.

This sometimes occurred with public service positions under the Comprehensive Employment and Training Act (CETA) in the 1970s, one reason why it fell out of favor. "Work" then becomes just entitlement aid under another name.

But for well-crafted experiments at the local level, those are dangers I would be willing to run—even more so if the programs are well evaluated so that we can learn something from them. Guaranteeing jobs—if the jobs make real demands—at least removes the excuse, which some non-workers make, that they cannot find employment.[4] The point of my conservatism has always been to make social programs less permissive, not to challenge the principle of helping the poor, or to economize.

ENTITLEMENT

The major point Mary Jo raises is about entitlement, which I take to be the core issue in welfare politics. The question is whether society must guarantee some minimal sustenance to the poor simply because they are needy, without demanding good behavior. Mary Jo sees in the gospels a moral injunction to do this. In her words, "the community is obligated to provide basic levels of sustenance, health care, and education for all its members." Public education is not in question here; we both accept that. Other benefits are more at issue. The appeal of an ultimate safety net is real; it suggests that we could ban at least the worst forms of destitution simply by providing everyone with minimal resources with no question asked.

But several issues arise. One is whether existing programs already achieve this. TANF clearly has rejected entitlement. Yet other welfare programs have either weak work tests (food stamps) or none (Supplementary Security Income).[5] These benefits might still guarantee a minimal income. Like Mary Jo, I think that the food stamp program is a vital dimension of the safety net. I also think that it strikes a good compromise between stigma and accessibility for the recipients. I am, however, torn between stiffening its work requirements and leaving it as a lifeline for all. I am torn in a different way by SSI. Clearly, there should be public support for needy people who are disabled, but deciding who they are requires making difficult judgments. As with other poverty issues, policymakers must aim for good consequences, not simply do what feels good in the short run.

Until recently, SSI was overused by drug addicts, children, and aliens; in 1996 Congress limited their eligibility. Admission to the program, which is controlled by state agencies, may also have been lax. The disabled adults on SSI are supposed to be incapable of taking any gainful employment for at least a year. However, a majority of disabled recipients claim eligibility due to mental conditions, many of them judgmental.[6] Some single mothers faced with TANF work tests have transitioned to SSI. It appears that at least some of the current recipients are in fact ineligible or would be better off working. Some, indeed, may be working off the books, as was common on AFDC prior to PRWORA. The caseload might be reviewed for employability. Admittedly, an attempt to do this with disability benefits under Social Security in the 1980s provoked lawsuits and great controversy, to the point that the review had to be halted.

Mary Jo suggests that we should also have national guarantees for shelter and health care such as those we have for food, and that we do not. I agree in principle that we should; whether we do or not is less clear. It is true that the nation lacks a comprehensive health system that ensures care to all in the manner of European welfare states. The defeat of the Clinton health care proposal, which would have universalized coverage, was an embarrassment to many. But through Medicaid and the State Child Health Insurance Program (SCHIP), coverage of the poor and near-poor, especially children, is already extensive. Many of the poor who lack coverage are eligible for these programs but have not signed up, for reasons that remain unclear.[7] Some without coverage have refused it from their employers because they are unwilling or unable to pay the premiums. Most important, most of those who lack health *coverage* do not appear to lack actual health *care*, at least not when they most need it. Many go to hospital emergency rooms or receive other charity care. While this arrangement is inferior to formal coverage, the nation clearly comes closer to a health guarantee in fact than in form.

As to shelter, clearly public programs are more lacking, but the problem also is smaller. Perhaps 600,000 people are homeless at a given moment.[8] For most, the problem is not really housing per se but income. Many of the homeless are on welfare, so in reality homelessness is part of the larger poverty and welfare problems. Persistent cases often are seriously disabled by substance abuse or mental illness. They are the most miserable of the poor, and society's obligation to them is clear. New York City, however, is the only locality that guarantees shelter to all needy people. This is due to legal settlements that rest, in part, on the New York state constitution, which mandates protection for the needy. But other cities have more limited shelter systems, and others rely on charitable organizations to fulfill a similar function. Often, the homeless people who remain on the streets have refused the aid that was offered to them. So the United States may lack a formal shelter guarantee, yet very few Americans, it appears, *have* to be homeless.

Deeper Issues

As these cases suggest, one issue raised by job programs and also by entitlements is how explicit the public role has to be. After all, the poor as well as other Americans receive most of what they need to live from the private marketplace. Most people receive income from private employment, then use it to purchase food, clothing, and shelter from private vendors, without any direct government involvement. These necessities are not guaranteed in any explicit way, yet they materialize every day for most people, including many poor. Is the maintenance of this structure a sufficient discharge of government's commitment to the needy?

If the private market does not provide, can the nonprofit sector be counted on to do so? Some have argued that the charity of the nineteenth century was more effective against poverty than today's public programs, just because it was private.[9] The conventional view is that private charity was overwhelmed by the Depression and that it can never meet the needs of today's poor population. But the charitable sector is much larger and richer today than it was a century ago, while the poor population—at least by the official measure—is smaller. Nonprofit involvement in antipoverty efforts is already extensive, especially in the largest cities and the older parts of the country.

If we assume that some public programming is needed, what level is adequate? Federal social programs express the most serious national commitments, and they seem to be what Mary Jo has in mind. My own preference, expressed in my response to Mary Jo, is that the most important social benefits and obligations should be national, because of their implications for citizenship. But if provision is reasonably uniform, using local

159

programming has advantages, as the implementation of welfare reform has shown. It facilitates innovation, competition among jurisdictions, and perhaps greater progress over time. It is also more consistent with the Catholic ideal of subsidiarity.

The larger reality is that, in an affluent society, there are many sources of income and support for the needy, not only government. Research has shown that poor families draw income from many sources, including public programs but also occasional work (often off the books), contributions by absent spouses, and help from friends and neighbors.[10] These sources help to explain why, as I mentioned in my opening essay, many poor people appear to consume at a level well above their reported income. Multiple sources of income also explain why the dramatic fall in the TANF rolls has not produced more hardship.

Another issue is what type of aid is required to create an entitlement. We tend to assume that entitlements mean benefit programs that deliver income directly to the recipients, but institutional care is an alternative. The final guarantee for children, the least controversial of the poor, is the child welfare system. Even if government refuses aid to parents and they cannot cope, it will place their children in foster care. It also will institutionalize substance abusers or the mentally ill. New York's shelter guarantee is another institutional solution. The homeless are offered a place to stay, rather than a stipend or food stamps, although they may receive those too.

But of course, institutional aid may do little more than keep body and soul together, and it denies those aided some of their liberty. Historically, one rationale for this approach was to make aid unattractive, so that fewer poor people would prefer to claim it than fend for themselves. This was what welfare reformers of the nineteenth century called "lesser eligibility." They wanted to limit public aid to "indoor" relief—support within institutions such as poor houses. Modern advocates of entitlement demand what the older reformers called "outdoor" relief—subsidies to support the poor in their own homes. Aid in this form allows them to live reasonably normal lives.

One question is whether it is practicable to do this. Outdoor relief assumes that those aided are unable to work. Are they then able to run their own households? Some opponents of recent welfare reform argue that welfare mothers often lack the capacity to work. Can society then trust them to raise children without oversight? For the more disordered of the poor, this question must be taken seriously.[11] The other question is fairness. Is it fair to the nonpoor to expect them to support needy parents in a normative life without demanding that they work, as the nonpoor themselves must? The public and its leaders have clearly rejected this demand for most welfare mothers.

The more searching question Mary Jo raises concerns not the extent or nature of aid guarantees, but whether entitlements are the best way to help the poor at all. We generally assume that to help the poor is to give them support. I would agree when the recipients are victims of misfortune, such as those bereft by September 11, or when they are clearly unemployable but still able to live independently. But in other cases, some other form of help may be better. The only response clearly forbidden by the gospels is indifference.

As I stated in my opening essay, the gospels suggest that Jesus had three goals for the poor, not only sustenance but community and autonomy. With some people he emphasizes one goal, with others another. Mary Jo cites the parable of the Good Samaritan, in which the good neighbor clearly is the person who offers sustenance without judgment. But there is also the man at the Pool of Bethesda who declined to accept responsibility for himself. Jesus tells him stand up and fend for himself. Jesus is still involved, still in relationship with him. He still helps; he does what the man needs most. Government, I think, acts similarly when it offers the needy work rather than aid or when it combines aid with definite demands to function.

While I agree with Mary Jo that there should be some entitlements, I am more open to the idea that they are already provided by the public or private sector, or might be provided in an institutional form. I also am more ready than she is to take risks with sustenance in order to pursue community and autonomy. I am willing to deny cash aid to the employable if doing so is necessary to enforce work requirements or perhaps some other civilities, although I would want some in-kind minimum still to be available to families. Welfare reform took exactly this kind of risk— enforcing work and driving many families off the rolls to promote work. Some may find the moral costs of that prohibitive. But the gains in employment, earnings, and social integration are clear. To me those also were moral priorities.

Why Theologians Go Unheard

The issues that Mary Jo has raised, particularly entitlement, are indeed the crucial ones surrounding poverty and welfare reform. I have wondered why a project like this was needed to bring religious perspectives to bear on such issues.[12] Given the obvious importance of poverty to society as well as our biblical tradition, one might expect heavy involvement by religious professionals (clergy and seminary teachers) in studying the problem and shaping public responses.

When the institutional church takes a public stance on poverty or welfare reform, its statements are written by staff who know the programs and issues. There are religious institutes that analyze important public issues, including welfare, and advocate positions.[13] There are some theologians who know a good deal about social policy and write expertly about it.[14] But in general, I have found the theological presence in the poverty debate to be surprisingly small. Scholars or advocates with roots in the professional church have not had a large influence.

One reason surely is that the nation's separation of church and state gives professional church people less standing to be heard on public issues than they enjoy in some other societies. So religion has real influence, but it comes chiefly through society's religious values, not through the church as an institution.[15] Another reason is that the generally conservative trend in social policy, and in politics, is uncongenial to most theologians, whose own politics, like that of other academics, tends to be left of center.

A third factor is that the poverty and welfare debate has become highly technical, due to the influence of economists and other social scientists who use statistical methods of analysis. One cannot maintain a standing in that debate unless one can at least read technical research and preferably do some of one's own. Few theologians have the taste, temperament, or training to do that. That partly explains why their empirical images of poverty often seem out of date. They often have not grappled with the lifestyle issues that secular experts on poverty take seriously.[16]

A more interesting reason, however, seems to be that many theologians have focused on issues that are remote from actual politics or policymaking. Many are preoccupied, for instance, with relating religion to the economy. Is property or wealth good or bad? Jesus and the prophets accepted possessions as good in themselves but saw covetousness as sinful. The early church fathers, who had a similar view, advised their followers to live frugally and to give the rest of their income to the community or the poor. Medieval monasticism treated the renunciation of property as an ideal, although it was not demanded of everyone. Protestantism affirmed the worldly callings of the laity, including money making, but could still be strongly ascetic.[17]

This debate lives on today. Ron Sider has restated the early church ideal in calling for western Christians to live on radically reduced incomes, the better to give much of their wealth to the poor, especially those in the starving third world. Conversely, John Schneider argues that God intended creation to be bountiful. Christians can and should enjoy wealth beyond the minimum, their duties to the less fortunate being limited mostly to people close to them.[18]

A related question is how the church relates to capitalism. The Bible portrays a world where moral judgments had authority over economic activity. In ancient Israel, debts were periodically remitted to protect debtors and a portion of harvests was reserved for the poor. In premodern Europe, monopolies, price controls, and prohibitions against usury restricted enterprise, often with a religious rationale. But rulers eventually came to view these restraints as corrupt. A deregulated economy was more productive and efficient. Adam Smith showed in 1776 that the pursuit of self-interest could be reconciled with the public interest by the market's "invisible hand."[19]

So western economies were progressively freed to steer themselves, denying theology its earlier authority. Economics was now a strictly secular subject with its own laws. Ever since, theologians have struggled to find some new way to make the biblical message relevant to economic life.[20] They resist the Smithian idea that collective good can best arise through the interaction of selfish intentions. They seek some new way for society to directly will and achieve the good.

One way churches have done that has been to support the quest since Smith to recontrol the economy, this time in the interest of the working class. The Catholic church took a moderate position in that struggle, accepting industrialism but insisting that property rights be subordinated to greater protections for workers and their families.[21] This issue too lives on. Liberation theology is a latter-day attempt to justify populist controls on world capitalism, which it says promotes dependency and inequality in poor countries. On the other side, conservative theologians argue that capitalism is a boon to the poor and a school of virtue.[22]

These issues may be theologically important, but in politics they are passé. In American public life, the value of wealth and capitalism is simply not disputed. At the same time, a large majority accepts that the economy needs some oversight by society, for moral and other ends. Long ago, the country settled on a mixed economy in which productive assets are privately owned but publicly taxed and regulated. There is ongoing argument over the proper extent of controls, but there is no prospect of large changes in the reach of government. Some theologians, like other academics, are alarmed by the passion to cut taxes and dismantle regulation that emanates from the Republican right wing. They think this portends a repudiation of public oversight of the economy, a resurrection of absolute property rights. I find that fear exaggerated. No recent development in economic policy compares to the revolution in welfare. In continuing to fight Adam Smith, the theologians distract themselves from the actual issues in politics.

The Prophetic Voice

Another reason why theologians count for little in the poverty debate is the unsophisticated positions that they have often taken. While church professionals do not all agree, their dominant voice has been like that of the institutional church—the religious organizations that take public positions on poverty and other social problems. These bodies have long favored a liberal but permissive policy toward the needy—increasing benefits and programs but without setting clear expectations for the recipients. They have been sobered by the success of recent conservative policies, and some now accept the need to enforce work. But they continue to express a vision of the poor as victims deserving principally of solicitude.

This position carries little weight in the public arena today, and not only because politics has turned more conservative in recent decades. Experts too pay little attention to church positions. Religious advocates frequently propose new programs of a sort that have received poor evaluations in the past. One still can make a case for new efforts, but it must be carefully aimed at the places where programs have shown promise, where it can reasonably be argued that doing more might achieve more. Among those areas are several that Mary Jo speaks of—food stamps, EITC, and job creation programs. There still are secular advocates who make such arguments effectively in Washington.[23] I have not seen those speaking for the churches show a comparable expertise or patience.

One of the reasons for this is the prophetic stance the churches tend to take toward government. Like Jesus and the prophets, they position themselves as outsiders criticizing moral wrongs. The idea is that government is abusing or neglecting the poor in some way but is in denial about it. Critics outside the regime, however, can see what is going on and invoke biblical injunctions against it. The prophetic stance involves little debate. Rather, moral critics utter judgments, and the powers that be either accept or reject them. This position was understandable in biblical times, in a world where government was monarchical and unaccountable to the governed.

Since then, however, two millennia of political development have intervened. Today's regime is far more open to criticism from the press and many other sources. It is less corrupt. It also is yoked to society through the election of officeholders. The chance that injustices will go unnoticed is small. Much more likely, grievances will be open but debated. There will be arguments for responding and for not responding. On any important issue, there will be two legitimate points of view, sometimes more. What improves policy in such a setting is not the unilateral pronouncement of moral judgments, but expertise and discussion.

The biblical stance is to criticize the moral failings of individuals rather than impersonal structures. That style was fitting as long as government was elitist and untrustworthy. The polemics between the prophets and Israelite rulers in the Old Testament represent one elite at war with another. Modern government, however, is more accountable and trustworthy and also less elitist. The moral qualities of rulers as individuals probably count for less. In fact, in personal terms, today's politicians are probably more admirable than those of a generation or two ago. The main limitations of the regime lie rather in its institutional features, especially the fractious tendencies of our political culture and the detachment of most ordinary Americans from politics.[24]

Religious commentators on poverty often express suspicion of the public. It is said that the voters are indifferent to the needy, or that the poor are powerless in a political arena where everyone else has more resources. Actually, polls show that voters are strongly committed to public antipoverty efforts, provided that programs are effective. And while low-income people would have more influence if they voted more, they are spoken for by many of the better-off. Their treatment is accepted as a moral touchstone for the regime, just as the Bible assumes, even if policy falls short in some ways. Theologians and some other academics also suggest that we cannot be candid about the lifestyle aspects of poverty, lest we undermine what public support for the poor there is. I think, rather, that a refusal to be candid long undermined support. Our current policies, because they are more realistic, are also much more popular.

Government needs prophetic chastisement less today than in the past precisely because it takes past chastisements to heart. Before 1960 the poor may have been, in Michael Harrington's words, the "other America"—unseen and ignored.[25] Since then, poverty has become a vital and ongoing focus of domestic policy. The taxes Americans pay to support social programs might well count toward the tithe that the Bible calls on believers to pay out of their income toward supporting the poor. Policymakers and experts labor earnestly and continuously to improve antipoverty programs. This situation calls for a less prophetic and more even-handed moral discourse. Mary Jo and I at least have attempted such an exchange in this dialogue.

Fairness

Neither the theologians nor Mary Jo and I have addressed well a final issue, that of fairness between rich and poor. Generally, the debate about helping the poor is about generosity rather than fairness. We ask how much the rich will do for the poor, as if only the actions of the rich mattered. I have argued here and elsewhere that the greater issue is reciprocity—what to expect of the poor in return for aid. In short, what the poor do also matters. Rich and the poor owe *each other* something. The issue is the *relative* obligations of the groups.

This question is neglected in our religious tradition, probably because it is largely overlooked in the Bible. Scriptures discuss how humans should relate to God and each other, but they offer no doctrine of distributive justice. Society's leaders are told to take care of the poor, and the poor are told, like other people, to behave well. But who should go first? If either fulfilled its obligations, there would be much less need for the other to do so. Who should bear burdens for whom? This question is not addressed. To generate a doctrine of justice, one always has to add some secular theory or ideology to the Biblical injunctions.[26]

So the liberal church can levy the entire responsibility for poverty on society, and within the biblical tradition there is little basis to resist. Religious advocacy for the poor often can be quite hostile to the rich. The urge sometimes seems to be to expropriate them, to have the first be last and the last first—in this world as well as the next. Ron Sider, for example, says he is not against the rich, but he also says that "rich Christians who neglect the poor are not the people of God." In religious terms, they are outside the pale.[27] But on this one-sided basis we cannot achieve community, which is one of the chief goals Jesus has for the poor in the gospels.

A related need is to address the psychic dimension of poverty. I have argued that the expansion of antipoverty programming in the 1960s and 1970s involved a broader redistribution of moral responsibility away from the poor and other victimized groups toward society. At a rhetorical level and in social policy, the disadvantaged were no longer held accountable for good behavior. This was unfair to the better-off, and again it is a barrier to integrating the poor.

We understand redistribution too much in material terms. Today's class system is more psychic than economic. If the rich are the competent and the poor the incompetent, then no redistribution of resources can overcome poverty. The rich could give everything they have to the less fortunate, and the latter would still look to them for solutions, remaining dependent forever. Sometimes, what the poor or their advocates seem to want most is not some material benefit but the right to complain, and it is this right that must be questioned. Sometimes I envy the poor. If I were like them, I could stop being responsible and complain myself. I want to say to them, "Take everything I have. Even take my job, my most prized possession—but you must stop complaining and accept the same responsibilities that I do!"

The Bible fails to address competence and responsibility because it is not sociological in the sense that I use the word. In Scripture, neither God, Moses, nor the prophets exempt people from accountability for their personal behavior. Jesus forgives people generously, but he also expects them to repent, and he affirms the law. His fabled solicitude for the poor occurs against the backdrop of a legalistic system of ethics, most of which he never questioned. Today, we have to rebuild these assumptions affirming personal responsibility, and we have to do it in the psychological terms that society now understands.

How we might do this is suggested by Paul Tournier, the only theologian I know of who has grappled with this inner dimension of inequality.[28] The essence of the psychic class system appears to be that the poor or their advocates are conscious only of their weakness, the establishment only of its strength. Each side projects its denied self onto the other. The poor attribute to the rich some of the competence that they could claim, while the rich project onto those they help some of their own vulnerability. Much of the bitterness over poverty results from the hunger each side feels for its denied self. The poor resent their inability to be masterful, the rich their inability ever to lay down their burdens. The *ressentiment* that Nietzsche blamed on Christianity is really the politicized envy of the strong by the weak.

Tournier says that community becomes possible only when the projections are withdrawn. The weak must reappropriate their strength and the strong their weakness. That requires that the poor become able to shoulder at least some norms of good behavior, what the Bible calls the law. And the rich must acknowledge their inability to do all that the law commands. As much as the poor, they need to be forgiven. Tournier specifically rejects masochistic conceptions of virtue that require the strong to immolate themselves on behalf of others. The identities of strong and weak are really idols that we must cease to worship. In political terms, the society must give back to the out groups some of the responsibility that it has assumed for them, and they in turn must become people on whom others can rely, at least in some respects. Only when our assumptions about human nature become more uniform can trust grow. Only then will "every valley . . . be lifted up, and every mountain and hill . . . made low."[29]

Perhaps what is going on in social policy is a working out of these missing dimensions of theology. We are hammering out a distributive ethic where it is clearer than in the Bible what rich and poor must do for each other. Neither side can now be called on to bear the entire burden of solving social problems. And in the process we are undoing the hidden psychology of poverty. The restoration of a common citizenship means that henceforth we can assume something more like the same basic competences and responsibilities for everyone. We can return to the less distressing economic meaning of class, where the rich merely have more money than the poor, rather than a different identity. That sort of inequality is a lot easier to deal with.

Notes

1. U.S. Census Bureau, March 2002 Annual Demographic Supplement, tables 10 and 13.

2. John C. Weicker, "The Labor Market Movie," *American Outlook* (Winter 1999), pp. 51–53.

3. Lawrence M. Mead, *Beyond Entitlement: The Social Obligations of Citizenship* (New York: Free Press, 1986), chapter 3.

4. Christopher Jencks, *Rethinking Social Policy: Race, Poverty, and the Underclass* (Harvard University Press, 1992), pp. 127–28.

5. SSI encourages work by recipients, and it can require recipients with substance abuse problems to enter treatment, but there are no work requirements of the sort seen in TANF.

6. In 1999, 11 percent of disabled SSI recipients ages eighteen to sixty-four were deemed eligible due to schizophrenia, 25 percent due to mental retardation, and 23 percent due to other psychiatric disorders. See House Committee on Ways and Means, *2000 Green Book: Background Material and Data on Programs within the Jurisdiction of the Committee on Ways and Means*, 106th Cong., 2d sess., 2000, Committee Print 106–14, 248.

7. One likely reason, mentioned above, is that some of those eligible leave Medicaid unnecessarily when they leave TANF; another is that they cannot manage the bureaucratic demands of maintaining eligibility and ties with providers; they find it easier to go to emergency rooms.

8. The upper bound of an Urban Institute estimate published in 1989 was 600,000 on a given night. See Martha R. Burt and Barbara E. Cohen, *America's Homeless: Numbers, Characteristics, and Programs That Serve Them* (Washington: Urban Institute, July 1989), chapter 2. There apparently is no later estimate.

9. Marvin Olasky, *The Tragedy of American Compassion* (Wheaton, Ill.: Crossway Books, 1992).

10. Kathryn Edin and Laura Lein, *Making Ends Meet: How Single Mothers Survive Welfare and Low-Wage Work* (New York: Russell Sage Foundation, 1997).

11. Neil Gilbert, "The Unfinished Business of Welfare Reform," *Society*, vol. 24, no. 3 (March/April 1987), pp. 5–11.

12. What follows is based on my limited reading in theology and interaction with theologians. My contacts include several conferences where I debated theologians (typically more liberal than I) about welfare and poverty, the Center for Public Justice project cited below, and discussions with religious academics, especially at Princeton Theological Seminary during 1994–96 and 2001–02, when I was at Princeton University. I am especially indebted for guidance to Max L. Stackhouse, who is Caldwell Professor of Christian Ethics at Princeton Theological Seminary and a personal friend.

13. Notably, the Institute for Public Justice in Washington, D.C. One of its products was Stanley W. Carlson-Thies and James W. Skillen, eds., *Welfare in America: Christian Perspectives on a Policy in Crisis* (Grand Rapids, Mich.: Eerdmans, 1996), to which I was a contributor.

14. See, for example, Michael Novak and others, *The New Consensus on Family and Welfare: A Community of Self-Reliance* (Washington: American Enterprise Institute, 1987), and Warren R. Copeland, *And the Poor Get Welfare: The Ethics of Poverty in the United States* (Nashville: Abingdon Press, 1994). Novak is a conservative theologian, Copeland a liberal religion professor.

15. Lawrence M. Mead, "Religion and the Welfare State," in Richard F. Tomasson, ed., *Comparative Social Research: The Welfare State, 1883–1983*, vol. 6 (Greenwich, Conn.: JAI Press, 1983), pp. 52–53.

16. Robert Benne, "The Preferential Option for the Poor and American Public Policy," in Richard John Neuhaus, ed., *The Preferential Option for the Poor* (Grand Rapids, Mich.: Eerdmans, 1988), pp. 53–71.

17. Justo L. González, *Faith and Wealth: A History of Early Christian Ideas on the Origin, Significance, and Use of Money* (Eugene, Ore.: Wipf and Stock, 1990); Max Weber, *The Protestant Ethic and the Spirit of Capitalism*, trans. Talcott Parsons (Scribner's, 1958); Michael Walzer, *The Revolution of the Saints: A Study of the Origins of Radical Politics* (New York: Atheneum, 1968), chapter 9.

18. Ronald J. Sider, *Rich Christians in an Age of Hunger: Moving from Affluence to Generosity* (Nashville, Tenn.: W Publishing, 1997); John R. Schneider, *The Good of Affluence: Seeking God in a Culture of Wealth* (Grand Rapids, Mich: Eerdmans, 2002).

19. Adam Smith, *An Inquiry into the Nature and Causes of the Wealth of Nations*, ed. Edwin Cannan (New York: Modern Library, n.d.).

20. Max L. Stackhouse, "What Then Shall We Do? On Using Scripture in Economic Ethics," *Interpretation*, vol. 41, no. 4 (October 1987), pp. 382–97; Allen Verhey, *Remembering Jesus: Christian Community, Scripture, and the Moral Life* (Grand Rapids, Mich.: Eerdmans, 2002), chapter 12.

21. Leo XIII, Rerum Novarum: *On the Condition of the Working Classes* (Vatican City, May 15, 1891).

22. Gustavo Gutiérrez, *A Theology of Liberation: History, Politics, and Salvation*, trans. and ed. Sister Caridad Inda and John Eagleson (Maryknoll, N.Y.: Orbis Books, 1985); Schneider, *Good of Affluence*, chapter 1; Michael Novak, *The Spirit of Democratic Socialism* (Simon and Schuster, 1982).

23. Two examples would be Mark Greenberg of the Center for Law and Social Policy and Robert Greenstein of the Center for Budget and Policy Priorities, both in Washington, D.C.

24. Derek Bok, *The Trouble with Government* (Harvard University Press, 2001).

25. Michael Harrington, *The Other America: Poverty in the United States*, rev. ed. (Penguin Books, 1971).

26. Max Stackhouse, "Protestantism and Poverty," in Neuhaus, *Preferential Option for the Poor*, pp. 7–8.

27. Sider, *Rich Christians*, chapter 3.

28. Paul Tournier, *The Strong and the Weak*, trans. Edwin Hudson (Philadelphia: Westminster Press, 1963). See also Lawrence M. Mead, "Conflicting Worlds of Welfare Reform," *First Things* (August/September 1997), pp. 15–17.

29. Isaiah 40:4.

CONTRIBUTORS

Mary Jo Bane is the Thornton Bradshaw Professor of Public Policy and Management at the Kennedy School of Government at Harvard University. From 1993 to 1996, she was assistant secretary for children and families at the U.S. Department of Health and Human Services. She resigned from that position after President Clinton signed the 1996 welfare reform law. From 1992 to 1993, she was commissioner of the New York State Department of Social Services, where she also had served as executive deputy commissioner from 1984 to 1986. From 1987 to 1992, at the Kennedy School, she was a professor of social policy and director of the Malcolm Wiener Center for Social Policy. She is the author of a number of books on poverty, welfare, and families.

E. J. Dionne Jr. is a senior fellow in Governance Studies at the Brookings Institution and University Professor in the Foundations of Democracy and Culture at Georgetown University. He is a syndicated columnist with the *Washington Post* Writers Group and a co-chair, with Jean Bethke Elshtain, of the Pew Forum on Religion and Public Life. Dionne is the author of *Why Americans Hate Politics* and *They Only Look Dead*, and he is editor or coeditor of several Brookings volumes: *Community Works: The Revival of Civil Society in America; What's God Got to Do with the American Experiment?; Bush v. Gore; Sacred Places, Civic Purpose;* and *United We Serve: National Service and the Future of Citizenship*.

Kayla M. Drogosz is a senior research analyst for the religion and civil society project at the Brookings Institution, where her research interests include ethics, political philosophy, and the public purposes of religion. She is a coeditor of *United We Serve: National Service and the Future of Citizenship* and a coeditor for the Pew Forum Dialogues on Religion and Public Life. She received her degree from New College, continued her graduate studies in religion at Hebrew University and received an MPA from the Maxwell School of Citizenship and Public Affairs at Syracuse University. She served previously with the policy offices of United Jewish Communities and in the political section of the U.S. Mission to the United Nations.

Jean Bethke Elshtain is the Laura Spelman Rockefeller Professor of Social and Political Ethics at the University of Chicago. She is a member of the National Commission for Civic Renewal and currently serves as chair of both the Council on Families in America and the Council on Civil Society and as cochair, with E.J. Dionne Jr., of the Pew Forum on Religion and Public Life. Elshtain is the author of several books, including *Jane Addams and the Dream of American Democracy; Who Are We? Critical Reflections and Hopeful Possibilities; Democracy on Trial; Public Man, Private Woman: Women in Social and Political Thought;* and *Just War against Terror: The Burden of American Power in a Violent World.*

Lawrence M. Mead is a professor of politics at New York University. He has been a visiting professor at Harvard, Princeton, and the University of Wisconsin and a visiting fellow at Princeton and at the Hoover Institution at Stanford. He has written several books, including *Beyond Entitlement, The New Politics of Poverty,* and *The New Paternalism.* Before going to NYU in 1979, he held several policy and research positions in and around the federal government. He testifies regularly before Congress on poverty, welfare, and social policy, and he often comments on those subjects in the media.

INDEX

AFDC program, 41, 42, 43–44, 62, 82, 88–89. *See also* TANF program

African Americans: middle-class growth, 84; poverty statistics, 27–28, 58; racial inequality model, 7, 29–32, 112. *See also* race issue

Aid to Families with Dependent Children (AFDC), 41, 42, 43–44, 62, 82, 88–89. *See also* TANF program

Antigovernment approach, arguments, 7, 86–88, 126–27

Autonomy goal, 76–78, 82–86, 94, 161–62

Bane, Mary Jo: biographical highlights, 3–4; perspectives summarized, 3, 4, 5–7; sections by, 12–52, 107–19, 140–52

Bartik, Timothy J., 39

Bishops' letter: arguments about, 16, 87; as Catholic social teaching, 14, 15, 146; work incentives/requirements, 92, 145

Bonhoeffer, Dietrich, 85, 86

Bush (G. W.) administration, 96–97

Canadian Self-Sufficiency Program, 47

Capabilities deprivation: New Testament views compared, 73; and policy assessment, 22–23; as poverty definition, 7, 19–22, 121–22, 142–43; and resource redistribution, 167–68

Capitalism. *See* market economy

Catholic sensibility: described, 17, 109; as policy analyst's perspective, 5–6, 14, 16–18, 146–47; in policy assessment, 22–23; as policy obstacle, 128–29; and treatment of welfare recipients, 42–43

Catholic social teachings: and immigration issue, 34–35; official nature, 14–15, 108–09, 146; as policy analyst's perspective, 5–6, 13–14, 27, 146–48; in policy assessments, 22–27; as policy barriers, 125–26; principles outlined, 15–16, 18, 39–40; and Sen's poverty definition, 20–22

CETA program, 38, 157

Charity. *See* mission to poor/oppressed

Children, poverty rates, 58, 61, 62
Clinton administration, 4, 91
Community: as antipoverty policy
   goal, 8–9, 161–62; in Catholic
   sensibility, 17, 128–29; entitlement
   program consequences, 82–86;
   New Testament teachings, 23–24,
   36, 73–76, 114–15; and psychic
   class system, 126–27, 168–69; and
   self-reliance approach, 88; as TANF
   program benefit, 93
Comprehensive Employment and
   Training Act (CETA), 38, 157
Congress, TANF reauthorization, 96–97
Consumption levels, 57
Cost effectiveness approach, 22
Culture of poverty, 4, 9, 66–68,
   121–22, 142–43

Developing countries, 20, 53–54, 57,
   63, 67–68
Devolution. *See* "local" principle
Dignity principle, 15, 24, 43, 92, 125–26
Disabled people, 27, 58, 157–58

Earned income tax credit (EITC),
   35–36, 40–41, 46, 130
Edelman, Peter, 4
Education, 20, 31–32, 37, 89–90, 124
EITC (earned income tax credit),
   35–36, 40–41, 46, 130
Elderly, 27, 35, 58, 60–61, 110–11
Employment. *See* work *entries*
Entitlement programs, 40–42, 81–86,
   114–18, 157–62. *See also* income
   transfer policies

Fair treatment issue, welfare reform,
   44. *See also* reciprocity approach;
   work incentives/requirements

Family formation issue, 45, 95–96,
   131–32
Federalism. *See* "local" principle
Female-headed families, 45, 58, 60, 62,
   93, 110–11
Food stamp program, 41–42, 115–18,
   131, 154, 157

Government intervention: Bible-based
   perspective, 79–81, 126; and capabilities deprivation theory, 22–23; as
   Catholic social teaching, 15–16;
   "local" principle, 43–44, 159–60; and
   self-reliance arguments, 86–88; and
   subsidiarity principle, 26–27
Greeley, Andrew, 17

Harrington, Michael, 166
Health coverage, 20, 37, 117–18, 158
Heclo, Hugh, 1
Hispanics, 27, 32–35, 132, 133
Homelessness, 158–59
Housing, 117–18, 123–24, 158–59

Immigrants, 27, 33–35, 64–65, 112,
   132–34
Incarceration rates, 28, 124
Income poverty: inadequacies as problem definition, 18–22, 57; statistics,
   19, 27–28, 35, 56–57, 58, 110. *See
   also* poverty problem, defining
Income transfer policies: and Christian
   tradition, 39–40; dignity principle,
   42–43; family formation issue, 42,
   45; "local" principle, 42, 43–44; time
   limits, 48; types, 40–42; work
   incentives/requirements, 42, 45–48.
   See also entitlement programs
"Indoor" versus "outdoor" relief,
   160–61

Institutional care, 160–61
Institutional church: defined/
  described, 14–15, 55, 108; entitlement programs, 82, 84, 87; on
  government responsibility, 73, 126,
  129; lobbying effectiveness, 148–50;
  on poverty causes, 63, 64, 67–68;
  priority of poor, 70, 144, 164–66;
  proposed role, 4–5, 150–51; TANF
  reauthorization, 97; work requirements, 91–92, 126, 144–45

Jesus, characterized, 127. *See also* New
  Testament teachings
Job creation policies, 38–39, 113–14,
  155–57
Job training, as antipoverty investment,
  37
John Paul II, 26, 93
Justice principle, 15

Lakoff, George, 127
Lasch, Christopher, vii
Liberation theology, 16, 63, 144, 164
Life expectancy, statistics, 28
"Local" principle: policy advantages/
  disadvantages, 128–29, 159–60; in
  policy assessment, 23; in self-reliance
  approach, 87–88; and subsidiarity
  concept, 6, 16, 26–27; TANF
  program, 42, 43–44, 129–30, 131
Loury, Glenn, 7, 29–32, 124–25
Luke (book of Bible), 12

Market economy: in Catholic social
  teaching, 15–16, 26; employment
  limitations, 36–37, 63; and job
  creation policies, 38–39; and mutual
  responsibility principle, 26–27;
  theology's struggles about, 163–64

Mead, Lawrence: biographical highlights, 4; perspectives summarized,
  3, 4–5, 8–10; sections by, 53–106,
  120–39, 153–69
Medicaid, 154, 158
Microcredit strategies, 39
Minnesota Family Assistance
  Program, 47
Mission to poor/oppressed: as Catholic
  social teaching, 15, 114–15; New
  Testament teachings, 12–13, 24–25,
  70–78, 109, 114–15, 125–26; in
  policy assessments, 23; secular
  traditions, 25–26
Mutual responsibility principles,
  22–27. *See also* reciprocity approach

New Testament teachings: autonomy,
  76–78; community, 73–76, 114–15;
  discipleship, 143; government
  responsibilities, 79, 122–23; and
  immigration issue, 34–35, 132; limitations for policy, 145–46; mission to
  poor/oppressed, 12–13, 24–26,
  70–71, 109; mutual responsibility,
  23–24; as policy analyst's perspective, 8–10; sustenance priority,
  71–73
New York City, 156, 159
Nonmarital births, 45, 59–60, 62, 95,
  124
Nonworkers: "deserving" versus
  "undeserving" labels, 57–58; poverty
  distribution, 27, 28, 35–37, 60–61,
  110–11, 153–54. *See also* poverty
  problem, defining
Novak, Michael, 16
"Nurturant parent" versus "strict
  father" models, 127

Obligation to the poor. *See* mission to poor/oppressed

Outcome-based policy as government responsibility, 80–81

"Outdoor" versus "indoor" relief, 160–61

Out-of-wedlock births, 45, 59–60, 62, 95, 124

Parenting models, comparisons, 127

Paternalism strategies, 9–10, 90, 122, 136

Policy analysis: Catholic sensibility perspective, 5–6, 16–18, 146–48; evaluation approaches, 22–23; New Testament perspective, 8–10; role of moral framework, 13–14, 53, 134–37

Policymaking and theologians, 8, 55, 162–66

Politics of poverty, 68–70, 82–83, 135–36

Pool of Bethesda story, 76

Poverty problem, defining: as capabilities deprivation, 7, 19–22, 111, 121–22, 142–43; culture argument, 9, 58–60, 62–68, 70, 121–22, 142–43; "deserving" versus "undeserving" labels, 57–58; as income level, 18, 19, 56–57, 110–11; politicization of, 68–70, 82–83; racial dimension, 7, 27, 28–35, 58, 112, 123–25; and work rates, 60–62, 153–54. *See also* mission to poor/ oppressed

Primus, Wendell, 4

Privatization issue, 43–44

Property rights, 15, 24

PRWORA. *See* TANF program

Public policy–religion, dialogue purposes/benefits, 1–3, 10, 148

Race issue: and culture argument, 65, 123–25; Loury's inequality model, 7, 30–32, 112; poverty statistics, 27, 28, 58; taxicab example, 30. *See also* immigrants

Rawls, John, 24, 25

Reciprocity approach, 8–10, 88–94, 126–27, 166–69

Religion–public policy, dialogue purposes/benefits, 1–3, 10, 148

Responsibility for the poor. *See* mission to poor/oppressed

Responsibility: for contributing to society, 39–40, 126; redistribution of, as entitlement program consequence, 82–86, 167–68

SCHIP (State Child Health Insurance Program), 158

Schneider, John, 127–28, 163

Schwartz, Joel, 66

Self-confirming racial stereotypes, 7, 30–32, 124–25

Self-reliance arguments, 4, 86–88, 126–27

Sen, Amartya, 7, 19–20, 21, 73, 121–22

Shklar, Judith, 7, 8–9

Sider, Ron, 11, 70–71, 163, 167

Small business development, 39

Social insurance policies, 40, 81, 155

Social Security, 40

Social teachings. *See* Catholic social teachings

Sociologism, 64, 66, 83, 141–42

SSI (Supplemental Security Income), 157–58

State administration. *See* "local" principle

State Child Health Insurance Program (SCHIP), 158

Subsidiarity principle: and government intervention, 6, 16, 26–27; and policy assessment, 23; and TANF program, 42, 43–44. *See also* "local" principle

Supplemental Security Income (SSI), 157–58

Sustenance goal, 71–73, 88, 93, 157, 161–62

TANF program: and dignity principle, 42–43; family formation issue, 42, 45, 95, 131–32; and "local" principle, 42, 43–44, 129–30, 131; poverty statistics, 28; reauthorization issues, 96–98; as reciprocity approach, 95–96, 154–55; and self-reliance approach, 95–96; statistics, 35, 41, 42, 92–93; work incentives/ requirements, 42, 45–48, 89–90, 132, 144–45

Taxicab example (racial stereotyping), 30

Temporary Assistance for Needy Families (TANF). *See* TANF program

Theologians and policymaking, 8, 55, 162–66

Time limits (welfare benefits), 48, 95

Tinder, Glenn, 3

Tournier, Paul, 168–69

Unemployment insurance, 40, 155

United Nations Development Program, 20

Wage levels, 37, 63, 65, 123

Wage subsidy programs, 39

Welfare. *See* AFDC program; TANF program

Whites, poverty statistics, 27–28, 58

Wisconsin, 156

Work incentives/requirements: EITC program, 35–36, 40–41, 46, 130; food stamp program, 116–17, 131; institutional church response, 91–92, 126, 144–45; as reciprocity approach, 88–94; TANF program, 42, 45–48, 89–90, 95–98, 132, 144–45

Working poor, poverty distribution, 27, 35, 37, 60, 65

Work opportunities: and capabilities deprivation theory, 22; and culture argument, 64–66, 155–56; government roles, 37–39; and market economies, 36–37, 63

Work rates, 60–62, 93, 123–24, 153–54